Walking with God

To Lisa
With best
wishes and
Christian Love

i

Published by Crossbridge Books
Worcester
www.crossbridgeeducational.com
© Crossbridge Books 2020

ISBN 978 1 8380028 4 8

British Library Cataloguing in Publication Data
A catalogue record for this book is available from the British Library

*All proceeds from the sale of this book will be used to further the
mission of Crossbridge Books to publish Christian literature*

Also published by Crossbridge Books:

**DIVINE HEALING, DELIVERANCE, AND THE
KINGDOM OF GOD** by Trevor Dearing

TOTAL HEALING by Trevor Dearing

GOD AND HEALING OF THE MIND
by Trevor Dearing

**MEDITATE AND BE MADE WHOLE THROUGH
JESUS CHRIST** by Trevor Dearing

THE LIVING WORD (daily readings from the psalms)
by Trevor Dearing

THE GOD OF MIRACLES by Trevor and Anne Dearing

CALLED TO BE A WIFE by Anne Dearing

Walking with God

by

Rev Trevor Dearing MA BD

Retired Anglican Clergyman, Itinerant world-wide
Minister of Divine Healing and Deliverance

A companion book to Divine Healing, Deliverance and the
Kingdom of God; a compendium of the Christian life

ACKNOWLEDGEMENTS

I want to dedicate this book to Elizabeth Young for her encouragement to me to return to ministry.

Also I want to thank my wonderful Christian family of Philip, Rebecca, Ruth and Rachel for their constant love of their eighty-seven-year old father, and their encouragement for me to continue to write.

My thanks go to Alison Faircliffe and now Heather Shead for typing the manuscript despite my many blunders. I want to thank my son-in-law Richard for designing the wonderful cover.

I also want to thank my prayer partners who pray for me every day as this is very important for me to know. I would especially like to thank those who have been in close contact with me for urgent prayer and encouragement, the Rev. Daniel Foot and his wife Kirtina, Pastor Brian Hanant and his wife Heather, John Webb, Jill and Stephen, Peter and Pauline Ellis, and Tricia Moore.

I want to thank especially Dr Ruth Price-Mohr for her very hard work in editing and publishing this book, as a Christian publishing company who are evangelical Bible believers.

CONTENTS   *Page*

PREFACE

Dear Reader,

I am writing as a retired Church of England clergyman aged eighty-seven. I have been in full-time Christian service for over sixty years. I have written over fourteen books particularly about divine healing of the body and the mind; I still live mostly by faith and all the proceeds go to Crossbridge Books ministry. I am writing in the hope that you will find this book very helpful as you journey through life. Obviously I have been through many experiences in my long life, some of which I share in ways which will, I hope, help you also. Where helpful, I also quote some extracts from the Bible, which I believe is the best guide to life there is. I am not writing with any aim to convert you to Christianity, and you may believe in another religion, have some faith, or none at all. I hope this book is a personal letter to you and will speak to you whatever your circumstances or age.

Yours sincerely

Rev Trevor Dearing MA BD

INTRODUCTION

I have entitled this book *Walking* with God because in my nearly lifelong experience of God and subsequent study of His ways in the Bible' I have found that He is never in a hurry to do what He wants to do, but will do things at the time He wants to do it.

It is certainly true that He sometimes goes before us, for example to prepare the way forward, and that He sometimes follows after us, maybe to put right our mistakes or even to clean up the mess we made of our living. It is certainly true that He is always with us in the present, as for instance when we pray. The Bible says He dwells in eternity, which by definition is above and beyond our time span.

Jesus (God) is said to be the Alpha and the Omega. In Greek this means the beginning and the end. He is said to be at the beginning and the end at the same time, which is hard for us to understand. A deaconess (Florrie Clark) I employed when I was vicar of St Pauls' Hainault, often said "God's timing is always perfect", and this I have found in my experience to be always true, although it isn't always seen to be true at the time.

So I believe, and you will see in this book, that God entered our time span when Jesus was born, coming from eternity to live and share human life in all its limitations. We remember His last words to

His disciples "I am with you always, even to the end of the age".

So I have found, although I did not begin life with any thoughts of God as I will share, this has always proved to be true for me.

PART ONE

Discovering God

Chapter 1

Discovering God in the midst of fear

It was on a Sunday lunch time, when I was suddenly overwhelmed with fear; it came upon me, as it were, from nowhere. I got off my chair at the dining table and stood shaking from head to foot with terror. I was aged eleven and my parents did not know what was the matter with me or what to do for me. I collapsed into an easy chair and mercifully the whole thing stopped as suddenly as it started. However, this was not the end of the situation but the beginning. These attacks of terror came upon me unexpectedly without explanation almost every day for eight years.

I also found that I had serious mental health problems. Wherever I was I had to sit on a chair near an open door so I knew I could flee at a moment's notice. Where I would flee to I didn't know. I was also in what my doctor called 'an anxiety state', constantly anxious about my health, worried about having a serious disease; obsessed with the thought of death or being buried alive. My fitful sleep at night was punctuated by nightmares. The year was 1944; my father was constantly excused army duty because 'his son urgently needed him at home'. My doctor tried several medicines to help me, one of which was called phenobarbitone, all to no avail. I was constantly absent from school and so I also grew physically weak and ill. This lasted until I was nineteen years of age, when suddenly I discovered the reality of God.

I had grown up in a good non-religious home where God and spiritual things were never mentioned. I shared my family's rather atheistic views, and of course never attended a church service. I have shared elsewhere[1] how I eventually joined a church youth club because I like playing table tennis, but absented myself from their nine o'clock epilogue session because I didn't want anything to do with religion. I have shared how it was when I went to my first church service that God, as it were, stepped out of the Bible and became real to me as I sat near the church door. It is hard to put religious experience into ordinary words, but in a moment of time, and in the midst of all the turmoil of my mental illness, I knew as sure as I was born that God existed; that He knew me and loved me.

In the Gospels, Jesus described the sudden and unexpected discovery of God's Kingdom as being like a man finding great treasure in a field, and in his joy and excitement, selling all he had to buy that field. Jesus also likened it to a man seeking precious pearls, who suddenly found a pearl of great price, and sold all he had to buy that pearl. My discovering God at that Methodist church in such a sudden and unexpected way certainly cohered with Jesus' two parables.

I have described the particular way in which way I came to faith in the God and Father of our Lord Jesus Christ. You will see that this was through suffering a great deal of emotional illness, which at the time was not understood or talked about.

People come to faith in as many different ways as there are people. For instance, my late wife Anne could never remember a time when she did not know God in a personal way, even when very young. In my experience, a lot of people come to faith when they are in desperate trouble and almost as a last resort. I have even helped prostitutes, alcoholics, drug addicts, and convicts come to faith.

My life has been dedicated to helping people, whatever their need or spirituality, and I hope I can help you. Some people go through life without discovering God at all which I think is very sad; thankfully it was not so for me as I found Him at the age of nineteen. So I have walked with Him in my life for sixty-eight years.

Chapter 2

Discovering God through the Bible

I certainly had a wonderful experience of God blessing me and healing me that evening in the Methodist church of Queen's Hall in Hull. I knew for certain that God existed, and that He knew I existed too, because He had answered my personal prayer. And I knew of course that as God, He had wonderful power, and had in a way undeniable to me, given me peace of mind. This was in the name, and through the invitation, of Jesus Christ who I thought immediately must be very closely connected to God, or even be somehow part of Him. So I had found the God who had made known Himself in Jesus Christ, and I'd found the God and Father with Jesus Christ His son. I certainly knew just these bare facts about God, but as I have said, it was enough to fill me with excitement and anticipation.

What did I need to do next? Obviously I needed to know and to learn as much about God as I possibly could and I knew that the main way of finding this out was to read it in the Bible, which I knew was closely associated with the Christian faith. So I actually bought a red New Testament which I well remember; it was small and it cost me in those days one shilling. So I started to read this book which, when I opened it, I realised I did not fully understand. I kept this copy of the New Testament in one of my pockets at all times in the ensuing months, and I used to grip hold of it in my pocket whenever I felt any sense of anxiety or fear. I found that when I said, whilst silently gripping it, 'Lord please help me', that immediately such fear, anxiety, and depression went straight away.

When I opened this little book, with its very small print, I found that the first chapter was about Jesus Christ, and it was the Gospel according to St Matthew. I went on to read the Gospels of Mark, Luke, and John, often in bed at night. Then I carried on with what's called the Acts of the Apostles, which I assumed was the message and ministry of Jesus' first disciples, now acting on their own with Jesus gone to Heaven, and I also came across the book of Revelation which I understood even less.

However, although I did not understand for example who the Philippians were, or who the Colossians were, I found God in the Bible - in the New Testament. From it I learned that God is indeed my Heavenly Father. I learned the Lord's Prayer, and I also found that God loves me. This was even more surely rooted in my mind than in the experience I had had in Queen's Hall. I got to know a lot about Jesus Christ and who He was, and I believed He was what He claimed to be, the Son of God, the Christ, Messiah. In the epistles I found some lovely thoughts about Jesus and what He had set out to be; that He had gone to Heaven and that now His disciples like Peter, Matthew, and John, were in a sense showing us what Jesus set out to do; His nature, His being, and His mission, and His sending out of the apostles as recorded in the Acts of the Apostles. About Revelation, it seemed to me to be in very strange language and ideas, but I did understand that as the final book of the Bible, it was proclaiming that in the end God would be, in Jesus, fully in charge, and all evil will be destroyed.

So I have explained how I came to know God from being an atheist, when I was expected to die before I was twenty-five, and how when I came to know Him, I was miraculously healed of emotional and physical conditions. I have also said that people get to know God in many different ways, almost as numerous as there are people, and there is absolutely no set pattern for this to happen. It is important to say, however, what we are discussing here is not just people coming to believe in God, which is very good, but going much further and having a real experience of God in their lives, and that experience is in fact life transforming.

So I'd had this experience of the reality of God which completely transformed my life. To quote the Bible, 'if any man is in Christ he is a new creation; all things have passed away, all things have become new'[2]. I certainly felt I was living an entirely new life, although I had of course connections with the old one. So taking the fact that people come to this experience of God, and a living

13

relationship with Him, in various ways, we now have to ask what sort of a God did I in fact come into a relationship with, who transformed my life, and what in fact was He like? Was He just a large, infinite blank in the sky? Or was He like what I was told, an 'unmoved mover'. Was He like the beliefs in the time of John Wesley, the sort of God who wound the world up like a clock and had left it to run its course taking no further interest in it? Or as Shakespeare envisaged, that all men are actors on a stage as it were, with God viewing with some interest what was going on?

I was told by my deaconess at the Methodist church where I was converted to Christianity, to study the Bible and find out all I could about God in the Bible. She said it would wonderfully enlarge my knowledge and my whole communication with this wonderful person who called Himself 'Jehovah', or in Hebrew 'I Am'. I had come to know Him through a sentence in Scripture in which Jesus said 'Come unto me, all who labour and are heavy laden and I will give you rest'[3]. So I realised, in a way that I couldn't understand fully, that Jesus and God were intimately connected, and even then I believed they were sort of all one. I saw that this God, in Jesus, made human beings like me, whatever their condition or state, to come to Him; a divine invitation, a wonderful invitation to a finite human being to come to the ineffable, almighty, victorious God. I also saw that this God would give a person like me rest, which I in fact experienced through that text of Scripture.

So He is connected with human beings in a wonderful way and is ready to meet their needs, and especially in my case my emotional needs. So following the deaconess' advice, I bought a little Bible, the King James edition. Nowadays there are so many different translations of the Bible, some of them only paraphrases not translating the exact original words. I find that now, as a mature Christian that can often speak the original Greek and Hebrew languages in which the Bible was first presented to mankind, I prefer to seek accurate translations. At the time of the Reformation in the 1500s, William Tyndale translated the Bible into English from the original Hebrew and Greek (rather than from the Latin), and in 1611 a version was published in English during the reign of King James, known as the Authorized Version. I now find the New King James edition of the Bible, as one understands the language, to be the best guide to knowing what the Bible really says.

Well, turning to the Bible, surely we can find God in the Bible easily because surely the Bible is all about God. Actually, the word Bible in Greek means a library and what I had in my hand in the King James Version was a library of books by up to sixty-six different authors and taking different points of view speaking about different things. So I learnt about God the creator in Genesis chapter 1. Then I found chapters 2 to 9 very difficult for a modern person to believe and understand, and I asked myself if they were fables passed on from generation to generation by Hebrew people over many centuries till they reached their present form? For the time being, I decided to pass by the literal meaning of those fables, but to try as I read them to see if there was anything they could teach me about the God I now had a relationship with.

Next I saw that, in what we call the Old Testament, or Old Covenant, which means the agreement that God made with the Israelite people; that He would be their God and had chosen them to be His special people to reveal Himself to, and make Himself known in His character and being to them. So that part of the Bible I found to be all about the relationship of God with the Hebrew people; setting them free from slavery to the Egyptians, with Moses leading them into what was called the 'Promised Land' of Canaan. Then God's dealings with His people were enumerated, outlined, and spoken about in the Bible; how they were taken captive, overrun by the Assyrian armies, with Jerusalem being destroyed in the year 622 BC, and some of the Hebrew people being taken away into foreign lands. The Assyrians were conquered by the Babylonians and the Babylonians were conquered by the Persians, and the Israelite people were taken away into captivity. Prophets like Isaiah and Jeremiah told about this coming to pass. Ezekiel addressed them in the foreign land and told them how to continue to live in relationship to God as His special people, because they were the remnant of the Israelite people, the rest having stayed back, being the weakest of them, in the area around Jerusalem.

All this was sort of a history of God warning His people that they would be punished for their disobedience to Him, having broken the law that Moses had given them in the name of God. Prophets like Ezekiel said that God would restore the remnant of His people, and that they would come back to their promised land, as many of them did as recorded in the prophesies of Nehemiah and Ezra. What in fact, I asked myself, could I learn about God from reading about His dealings and His relationship with this ancient people with their old covenant, a 'covenant of salt', an unbreakable agreement between God and them. Of course they didn't call it the old covenant; it was just, as it were, their Bible complete. The Hebrews referred to the books of the law as the Torah.

I can understand why people, even Christians, find the first seven books of the Bible something that is hard to believe, assuming that they are probably fables passed down from generation to generation. But a full search can still teach us a lot about God even if we do not accept their absolute existence in the world as historically accurate. I found that the Old Testament was about God's dealing with the Jewish people who He had chosen as a special race to make Him known to the world. I read the history of the Jewish people, with God as their Father, until they were taken captive by the Assyrians, then the Babylonians, then the Persians. I found that as I studied God's dealings with the Old Testament people, the Israelites, through all their vicissitudes, I found that God was real and I could learn a lot about Him, especially through prophets like Isaiah, Jeremiah, and Ezekiel. These prophets declared the word of God to the people of the time, and lovely passages come out of their writings such as 'But those who wait upon the Lord shall renew their strength; they shall mount up with wings as eagles, they shall run and not be weary, they shall walk and not faint'[4], and things like 'I know the plans I have for you, declares the Lord, plans to prosper you and not to harm you, plans to give you hope and a future,'[5] and 'Come now and let us reason together, says the Lord, though your sins are like scarlet, they shall be as white as snow; though they are red like crimson, they shall be as wool,'[6] and 'Thou wilt keep him in perfect peace, whose mind is stayed on Thee, because he trusts in Thee.'[7]

The Old Testament begins with the book of Genesis (the word genesis in Hebrew means beginning) which is a very important book. It also lays the foundation of all God's revelation - making Himself known to the human race. The first words of this book are the most important in the Bible 'In the beginning God'[8], and the majestic and inspired account of the creation of planet earth. It goes on to describe how God created man to commune with Himself 'in his image'[9]. A very important matter is the call of Abram (later called Abraham) to be the father of the Hebrew nation and ultimately of all Christian people. He is called the father of the faithful. In the Psalms, which were the hymns of the Temple, can be found wonderful verses about God being a rock behind which we can hide and shelter from the storms of life, and verses like 'In God will I trust; I will not be afraid what man can do unto me',[10] and 'Bless the Lord O my soul, and forget not all His benefits; who forgives all your sins; who heals all your diseases'[11].

Next I turned to the New Testament and found that the Gospels were all about Jesus and His life and His being, and all His miracles, and Him being declared the Messiah by some and rejected by others. And that He instituted a new covenant with a new people that would consist of nations and peoples and tongues (languages) other than the Jews; a new covenant by His sacrifice on the cross bringing the forgiveness of sins and the coming into being of a new people; all nations, kingdoms and tongues belonging to God as His new people. I found the epistles, that were letters written by prominent apostles like Peter and Paul, giving the meaning, or as we would say the theology, behind all Christ's life, death and resurrection, culminating in the book of Revelation and God's final triumph in the establishing of His kingdom in power. This was

19

the Bible the deaconess said that I should read to learn more about God.

In the New Testament of course, there are all the sayings of Jesus such as 'If anyone thirst let him come to me and drink,'[12] and speaking to a Samaritan woman, 'whoever drinks of the water that I shall give him will never thirst; the water that I shall give him will become in him a spring of water welling up to eternal life.'[13] Also verses like the one I found in my first encounter 'Come unto me all ye that labour and are heavy laden and I will give you rest. Take my yoke upon you and learn from me; for I am gentle and lowly in heart, and you will find rest for your souls. For my yoke is easy, and my burden is light.'[14] He made promises to the apostles when He was going away to Heaven, 'And when I go and prepare a place for you, I will come again and will take you to myself, that where I am you may be also.'[15] Wonderful verses like 'Cast all your cares upon Him, for He cares for you'[16]; 'Do not be anxious about anything, but in all things by prayer and supplication with thanksgiving make your requests known unto God, and the peace of God which surpasses all understanding, will guard your hearts and minds through Christ Jesus.'[17]

In Revelation we read these wonderful prophesies, 'Then I saw a new heaven and a new earth; for the first heaven and the first earth had passed away, and the sea was no more. And I John saw the holy city, the new Jerusalem, coming down out of heaven from God, prepared as a bride adorned for her husband,'[18] and it goes on to say God 'will wipe away every tear from their eyes, and death shall be no more, neither shall there be sorrow nor crying nor pain anymore.'[19] In Micah we read 'nation shall not lift up sword against nation, neither shall they learn war anymore.'[20]

As I looked at it, it seemed a rather awesome task for me to read this large book with many strange ideas and seemingly incredible things like a man being in a big fish's stomach for three days - his name was Jonah[21]; writing on the wall[22]; a donkey speaking[23] ; all sorts of things happening that were foreign to my understanding of the laws of nature of the planet Earth and its inhabitants. Again what could I learn about God from all this?

Some would think that by simply reading the Bible from cover to cover, or bits they liked, you would sort of automatically come to know all there is to know about God. Firstly, the Bible says that no man can ever know, certainly in this life, all there is to know about God. But in His dealings with the Israelites, and the Jews in the New Testament, God has shown Himself to be a God of love. As Jesus taught, our 'Father', or 'daddy' as it is in the Greek, loves and cares for us in the Christian life we should expect to lead, in our final entering into Jesus overcoming death, and in entering into life everlasting.

We have to acknowledge that a lot of people have read this whole book, or parts of it, and not come to any kind of belief at all or any kind of relationship with God. In fact, quite the reverse; they have found that reading the Bible led them to believe that there is no God. So, in recent times a professor at a university (Richard Dawkins) wrote a book called 'The God delusion' saying that there is no God, or certainly didn't seem to be a God. Even members of the Church seem to disbelieve the testimony of the Gospels, like the former Bishop of Durham who said that the resurrection of Jesus was just a bag of old bones and that there were no such things as kings or their like visiting Jesus at His birth. So also, it seemed that modern scholarship about the Bible, called higher and lower criticism, which I had to study later for my academic degrees in theology, also poured a lot of doubt on the truth of the Bible as proclaiming there is a God and what He is like.

So it is not just a matter of reading the Bible which will bring us a new knowledge of God or even to belief that there is such a person governing the universe. No, what matters in the end is not just reading the Bible as an ordinary book, but it is the way we come to the Bible to read it; with what attitude, whether we are seeking to disprove it, or searching through its many varied pages for the reality of God, His nature, and His dealings with the human race. This usually entails the fact that we are believers, or seeking to be believers, and if we come like that as I did, having had my experience of God, we certainly, as we read the Bible though not understanding all of it in the beginning, will come to a very deep and greater knowledge of the God we are experiencing. So we can pray to Him, because the Bible says He is intimately concerned with the welfare of the human race and each individual in it.

So I read the Bible. It took some time, but through it my knowledge of the God I had come to believe in, and was experiencing, was deeply enriched. I found Him to be not only the Father of the human race but to be my Father, with many promises given for Him to care for me and love me, and to seek my wellbeing. In fact the Bible, in one letter, said that I had been chosen by Him before the foundation of the world to be His child, along with myriads of others.[24]

So from that moment of time, when I came to know Jesus as one who would give me peace and healing in my mind and body, I have continually read the Bible, not just to criticise it, but with deep hunger and thirst, because the Bible says of itself in Paul's letter to Timothy[25], that every sentence in the Bible is what in the Greek says is 'God breathed'. In other words God inspired. It's a book given to us by God, not just dead pages like a novel, but real life in it which can, if we read it with hungry souls searching for God, find sentences and promises, and all sorts of things that will leap out of it into our hearts to

23

nourish our faith and our lives. We can find God in the Bible certainly, but we must come to it with a humble, even contrite approach, as creatures in search of the Creator. This reading of the Bible, in my case to the age of eighty-seven, is a life-long pursuit and a life-long learning.

So we read the Bible, and often need explanatory notes to understand it more fully, and many of these are available to Christians today, issued by various societies to help us in our understanding. Sentences from the Bible have been the subject or text of my sermons, always built on what the Bible says about this particular subject. The most important fact that we must learn from the Bible is what is called our 'salvation'. I, at the time I came to know Jesus, did not feel, in the usual terminology, 'convicted of sin'. I did not in fact feel a 'sinner' at all. Perhaps God let me off that feeling because I already had enough problems as it was. Certainly, if we are to approach God we must come with a definite need in our lives, because it's only when we feel a need, which will be variously felt by many people, that our various needs will be met in the words of the Bible and the experience of God.

The fact that I was a sinner, as I really was, came home to me over a period of two or three years, and until then I could not understand what all the tremendous emphasis on Jesus dying on a cross and rising again was really about, because He had to die somewhere, and certainly as He was God's son He would rise from the dead. But as I drew nearer to God and His holiness and purity, which the Bible taught me, I also found His love, especially in words like 'God so loved the world that He gave His only begotten Son that whoever believes on Him shall not perish but have everlasting life.'[26] (The Greek word for world is 'kosmos'; humanity in enmity against God) God so loved – in the Greek 'agape' a sacrificial love, totally giving, not thinking of itself at all, utterly, absolutely, laid out as it was on the cross. But I did see that Jesus had earned the forgiveness I received; paid the price of my sins, and it was through that death on the cross, trusting Jesus as Saviour and sacrifice and high priest, that my sins were forgiven, and that is the deepest peace of all. As the psalmist said 'Blessed is the man whose sins are forgiven, whose iniquities are taken away'[27] and the hymn writer 'O Love, Thou fathomless abyss, my sins are swallowed up in Thee; covered is mine unrighteousness, from condemnation now I'm free; since Jesus' blood, through earth and skies, mercy, free boundless mercy cries.'[28]

The Bible is often referred to as the 'Word of God', in other words, God speaking to the human race that He created. God teaching them through this 'in-breathed' book all they need to know about Him; all they need to know about their salvation; all they need to know about their relationship with Him; all they need to know about His care for them; all they need to know about praying to Him; all they need to know about who they are, why they are here, where they are going.

So I have described my rudimentary attempts to understand the Bible without having much background. Bible study deepened my convictions about the God of Christian faith and has been my lifelong pursuit through Bible College (Cliff College) and two universities (London and Birmingham). There I studied criticism of the Bible, that is about its authorship, date and so on, and lower criticism of the Bible, studying its coming into being in English from its origins for example in the Codex Vaticanus (one of the oldest copies of the Bible held in the Vatican library). This type of study can damage a Christian's faith, especially those who are new Christians. Jesus warns that those who cause others to stumble, even though it be through innocent-seeming academic study, come under the judgement of God.[29] If we become simply a scholar studying an ancient manuscript, without any other motive in mind, we shall not find God in the Bible.

As I have gone on in my Christian life till now, at the age of eighty seven, I can say I have never doubted the overall truth of the Bible and its meaning for people in every generation. Anybody who is searching for God can find Him in the Bible without having had such a religious experience as I had. There are apparently some people who have come to this kind of faith through reading the Bible. I remember hearing the testimony of David Suchet, who played the detective Poirot on TV, saying how he came to be a Christian through reading chapter 8 of the Apostle Paul's epistle to the Romans in his hotel room, when he had never had any belief before that, and having read it he had to rush out to try to find a book shop somewhere in the vicinity to buy a Bible. Yes, if we search diligently and sincerely, we shall find wonderful messages about God and who He is that will keep us going through all of our lives and give us hope for eternal life beyond the grave

Chapter 3

Discovering God amongst His people

When I had my wonderful experience of God meeting me, loving me and healing me, in Queen's Hall on that Sunday evening, I was alone except for a young lady who was sitting next to me who had brought me to the service. However, when the service was over, I found myself amongst a whole group of people about my age, from about eighteen to twenty-two years of age, probably about twenty-five of them, who had all been at the service. They told me that they all liked to go for a walk around the centre of Hull after the service before going home, and they kindly invited me, a stranger, to go with them. It was the first time I had really been out in a social way with a crowd of young people. I was aware that I was very thin and white-faced from my illness, and my face covered all over with acne, but thankfully they didn't seem to take any notice of that and we had a happy time chatting with one another about many things as we walked around the city centre.

One of the things I noticed, however, that was not talked about, was the evening service. Certainly there was no discussion about the sermon or mention as to whether it was helpful or good or boring. As I got to know these young people, after youth club as well as the service on a Sunday, I found that they really didn't have the experience of God in any way like I had. They seemed to be happy just to have the Epilogue as a religious act on Tuesday and Thursday evening at the youth club. It seemed to me that they were going to church because it was their family's tradition to do so and their mothers and fathers liked them to go to church, and certainly as I met one or two of their parents, I found that they were certainly Christians and had the same experience as me and could talk about God freely, and they were very happy.

So I continued with these young people, going to dances at the Bilton Home Guard, dancing with them until 11 o'clock. We kept ourselves very much to ourselves, and if I asked a young lady to dance with me I was never refused. A lot of these young people were in fact in couples; they had coupled up with boyfriend and girlfriend and had sort of relationships with each other in this way. I didn't have a girlfriend, so I was a bit of a way out in their eyes, and in fact I never did succeed in getting a girlfriend amongst that crowd of Methodist young people from Queen's Hall. We even went on holidays together to Christian Endeavour holiday homes.

I was becoming extremely proficient at table tennis and we belonged in a league of table tennis teams in Hull and I was Queen's Hall's number 1 player and was very successful, often being the winner. We climbed up the league table to be top of the league in Hull, and the rest of the team thought it was mainly through my joining them and my efforts. So I felt at home in that kind of way as well. Two ladies always came before 9 o'clock to make cups of tea. They were always there and loved to be amongst young people and never failed with their lovely cups of tea about half past eight in time for the Epilogue which everyone was supposed to attend at 9 o'clock. I used to make excuses to go out because I did not at that stage want anything too religious.

Then I found I was not only amongst a group of young people but amongst adults as well, because they were the parents of these young people, and I often went to their homes and they often had parties at the homes of these young people and I got to know the parents very well and was able to share my Christian faith with them. One such man was a man called Tom Fowler, an old and ardent Methodist Christian whose son Michael was my best friend, when he wasn't out with a girlfriend - he was very popular with the girls. He didn't have my experience of the Lord or the Christian faith, but Tom Fowler gave me a book of simple theology illustrating all the way through from Genesis to Revelation in easy language, in pictorial language, about what a Christian really should know about their faith, and I read it with great ardour. I admired Tom Fowler for his wonderful faith, especially when he lost a son aged five in a car accident outside his house, run over in the middle of the road, and Tom on the gravestone could write 'Thy purpose Lord we cannot see but all is well if done by Thee'. What faith, I thought, to surrender to God and His will in that way.

What I was now really a part of, and had become a member of, was a 'church'. I used to stay behind after the evening service to partake of Holy Communion, when in fact most of the congregation didn't bother to do it, and I felt it was a very important thing to do. Even the brass band that played before the service all went home with their musical instruments and didn't stay for the service itself. I felt all this was rather strange.

We did have instruction in the Christian faith. On Sunday afternoon there was a Bible class led by Sister Elisabeth Gillings in a very lovely way. It was open to discussion and nearly all the young people of the church went to it. I have had photographs even recently of that group meeting together in the home of one of the more wealthy young Christians (now a doctor), and they were all together just the same, except of course that I myself was missing because I was serving God in other parts of England. So this brought me to the study of the word 'church', because I was amongst God's children and they called themselves the Methodist Church.

In my companion book (Divine Healing, Deliverance and the Kingdom of God), I started by saying that Jesus came with the good news of the Kingdom of

God. A kingdom obviously involved a lot of people, and it became an assembly; a mass of people out of every race, tongue and nation; it superseded being the chosen people only of the Jews.

When I got to my theological studies, I discovered that the word translated as 'church' only occurred twice on the lips of Jesus, whereas as I have said in my previous book, the word 'kingdom' occurred several times and with deep theological meaning. The word church, I found in the Greek, meant something quite different from the way it is used today. In the Greek there was the suffix 'ek' added to the noun to make 'ekklisia' which means 'called out'. So the word translated as 'church', in the Bible, right the way through not only on the lips of Jesus, really could better be translated as 'the called out ones'. It certainly never referred to a certain building, because in any case Christians worshipped in houses until the conversion of Constantine which made Christian building legal; the Christian religion the religion of the Empire. It never referred in any way, this word church, to an institution of any kind. So the New Testament word for church was far removed from the concept of church that we have in our day when we say 'we are going to church', meaning that you are going to a building, maybe of a certain denomination. Such things, obviously, were not known in the early church. The word translated as church meant an Assembly of God's people who were 'called out' to belong to God, under His Kingship, and thus called out from belonging to the world of mankind.

Jesus gave a lot of teaching about how life should be lived within this Assembly of God's people, especially emphasising the virtue of humility; each counting the other as better than themselves. The Apostle Paul's epistle to the Philippians says how Jesus, though He was in the form of God and equal with God, made Himself with no reputation, being made in fashion like a man and dying on a cross,[30] and Paul goes on to bid other Christians to follow Jesus' example. Jesus, in one instance, had taken a bowl of water and a towel and washed His disciples' feet, taking on the form of the lowest servant in the household.[31] He said you know who I am, I am your master, yes but as I have done to you, do this for one another.[32] Obviously, Jesus' main 'cement' if we can call it that, for His Church, that was not limited to a city or a country but worldwide, His cement calling Christians together was to be love. He said 'Love one another as I have loved you,'[33] so we ought to love one another.

In my own life, I was obviously at first a member of the association of Christians which met at the Queen's Hall building in the city of Hull, but of course that Assembly was also wider, embracing all Methodists, in fact all Christians outside Hull and outside Yorkshire and covering the whole world of mankind.

The main reason why these Christians met together was to worship God and Jesus Christ. The word 'worship' means to ascribe worth, and all these Christians, in songs and hymns and prayers, were ascribing supreme worth to God our Father in Heaven. Anything that gets in the way of the supremacy of God - in between Him and His people, to be ascribed worth to, is in fact idolatry.

I quite soon became recognised as a Methodist Local Preacher, a man who knew quite a lot about the Bible, and I embarked on going out of Hull, out of that Assembly of Christians, into the wider world of Christian people. I did this by first becoming a student at Cliff Bible College in Derbyshire, where I met with young people who were much more deeply consecrated than those at Queen's Hall, so much so that I felt out-of-my-depth and a stranger, and worried about my own faith. But they were a wonderful bunch of men at that time and eventually I began to share the same faith as they had.

From there I went into the wider fellowship of Christians in Norfolk, still Methodist, where I became pastor in charge of ten rural churches and cycled twenty-five miles every Sunday, often in pitch black darkness, along country lanes, preaching three times on route to my lodgings. From there it was fellowship at Wesley Theological College, and then, as I felt my calling was more to the Church of England, as I hadn't been brought up a Methodist and very much liked the emphasis the

Church of England put on Holy Communion, the sacraments and the liturgy, I was ordained into the Church of England and attended Birmingham Theological College. At the Methodist College I obtained my Batchelor of Divinity, and at Birmingham I obtained my Master of Arts. All of this brought me into a very wide fellowship of Christian people of different persuasions of all kinds. So my Christian life was enriched by fellowship with them and this eventually became a worldwide field rather than the rather narrow Christianity of Queen's Hall in Hull.

This brings me to an analysis of the word 'fellowship', in the Greek 'koinonia'. Fellowship is in fact a deeper relationship with people than friendship. I rather liken it like this, to illustrate it I clench both my fists and put them together one by one bobbing up and down, that is a normal relationship that people have with their friends, but when I loose my fingers and entwine them together to form one; I have ten fingers closely related. This is how I conceive of the sharing of life in fellowship. This is what fellowship really means – belonging to one another at depth. John Wesley certainly had a very great vision of Christian fellowship, and the Methodists indeed had that fellowship, whereas many Anglicans went as single people, maybe as a family, to a building just to do their worship and go home until the next Sunday. So I enjoyed this fellowship that Charles Wesley summed up in a hymn 'He bids us build each other up, and gathered into one, to our high calling's glorious hope, we hand in hand go on.'[34]

So from the age of nineteen to my age now of eighty-seven, I have had wonderful experience of fellowshipping with some very deep, ardent, and encouraging Christians. Perhaps sometimes I have been used by God to build up their faith, and they certainly have been used to build up mine, because the church 'ekklesia' the 'called out ones' is indeed worldwide, and even where there are no buildings, or if the buildings are all destroyed, the 'koinonia', the fellowship, would still exist. So I have found God amongst His people.

I liken Christianity to an island of men and women set remotely in the seas, totally surrounded by water. On it these people all live, but they are all born blind. Then one of them has his eyes opened (we would say by the work of the Holy Spirit) and suddenly his experience becomes enriched and is absolutely dazzling with colours and trees and hills and mountains and snow, and he gasps for breath at the sight of this wonderful picture he has, at the sight before his eyes. He tries to tell other people on the island what he has seen; it is hard to find words to describe what he has seen because it's all so new and different. In fact as they listen to him they think he has become a lunatic. Then another man's eyes are opened and he says to the first 'why didn't you tell me it was as wonderful as this?' He says I've been trying to tell you but you wouldn't believe me. Then one by one all the eyes of the people on the island are opened and they are all astounded and wonder at their new surroundings, their new world; sharing a common experience, they form the church.

I certainly discovered God amongst His people when my spiritual eyes were opened as I too had the same experience as them, with whom I shared a common life in a wonderful way. My most wonderful experience amongst these people was meeting with Anne, with whom we found the deepest experience possible, whom I married in 1957 and we shared our common life and ministry together.

Chapter 4

Discovering God as Saviour

I had been attending worship at Queen's Hall in Hull for over a year and I had been attending a Bible teaching class for young people, saying private prayers daily, and was a very live member of the church, when as I was walking down a street, a man came up behind me and put his hand on my shoulder and asked "Are you saved?"

I did not know at all what he meant, but he had given me something to think about. The fact that God is our Saviour runs right through the Bible, and Jesus was actually given a name that means saviour. It was two years before I realised what an important question the man in the street had asked me. It is a vital part of Christian faith to be saved, not only important in this world, but also in the next. After having thought for a long time about this, I came to prefer the word 'rescue'. God's greatest work for the human race was to rescue it and also in saving us from our sin and its consequences: their lost eternity. Paul says in his letter to the Romans that 'all have sinned and fallen short of the glory of God.'[35]

Sin has been a complete barrier between man and God since Adam sinned in the Garden of Eden. This account of the fall of man shows that God did not make robots that would automatically obey Him, since He gave Adam, and all men and women, a free will to choose whether or not to obey their Creator. As a result of sin, they went entirely into isolation from God, as we can see from the state of the world today.

Paul writes, in Romans and again in 1 Corinthians, that by one man sin came into the world, and also death, but that by one man (Jesus) came freedom from sin, and life.[36] The Bible teaches that God's great act of rescue came about when Jesus died upon the cross. It is written that just before he gave up His spirit, he cried out "It is finished".[37] The words 'it is finished' in the Greek means it is completed or perfected; nothing can be added to it or taken from it without spoiling it. The way of salvation, or as I say, 'rescue', was absolutely and forever completed. As the Apostle Peter wrote, "As the outcome of your faith you obtain the salvation of your souls,"[38] and "He himself bore our sins in His body on the tree, that we might die to sin and live to righteousness."[39] Paul states in Romans, in the language of the courts, that we are guilty before God and His justice, and that Jesus Christ has paid the penalty for us.[40]

Perhaps you would think that claiming this great act was entirely down to us, but I called this chapter 'Discovering God as Saviour' because the Bible teaches that our salvation is the work of God Himself. In his letter to the Ephesians, the Apostle

Paul writes that we were individually chosen by God and predestined to claim our salvation before the foundation of the world.[41] By grace we are saved by faith, not works (good deeds), and this faith by which we claim our salvation, is itself the work of God.

So we can say to ourselves that once saved all was saved; we can be secure in our communion with God now and forever; that our salvation is not attained by anything we do, for example going to church, being baptised, praying, reading the Bible, or good deeds. In the Gospels, Jesus says to a very religious man "You must be born again to see the Kingdom of God."[42] This man was called Nicodemus, a very righteous man. Later, Jesus told a parable about two men who went up to the Temple to pray; one a Pharisee was a very religious man who kept the law of Moses to the letter; by contrast, the other was a tax collector, a sinner. Jesus said it was the tax collector, who cried out to God to have mercy upon him, who was justified.[43]

In all this we see that not everyone who attends church regularly, or who loves to do good deeds, is necessarily a child of God. If they are trusting in these things for salvation, they will go to a lost eternity because they do not realise that God alone can actually rescue them from their sins. So we see that God takes the initiative from beginning to end in our salvation, so as we walk with Him, He leads us into salvation, and it was as I walked with God for two years that at Cliff College I walked to the front of the church, led by God to claim my salvation, shedding many tears, then walking with God in a deeper peace and joy than I had ever known before.

We come to this point in different ways, according to how God leads us, so my late wife Anne told me that she had known God all her life, in a personal way, from being a young child. She actually claimed her salvation at Ketton Methodist Church near Stamford when she was sixteen years of age, when she was the only person to answer the 'alter call' issued from the pulpit by a young man. Her journey to salvation was different from mine, and I have heard hundreds of people saying how they came to salvation, many of whom have been instrumental in bringing people like Anne to God. We worship God, attend a church, are baptised, have private prayer times, tell others of our experience of God, do many good works – not in order to be saved – but because we are already saved. A very important text in the Bible is perhaps the most important verse ever written in John's Gospel: 'God so loved the world that He gave His only begotten Son that all who believe in Him should have eternal life. For God did not send His Son into the world to condemn the world, but that the world through Him might be saved.'[44]

So I ask, dear reader, as the man in the street asked me, "Are you saved?"

Chapter 5

Deepening your experience of God

When you have had an experience of God revealing Himself to you, in whatever way, whatever time or place, it is perhaps the most precious experience you can ever have in this life. However, if like me you have had no Christian upbringing or instruction, you would find that it is definitely needed to deepen your knowledge of God in the same way as for example when you are married you need to deepen your experience together as husband and wife; what you really are as a person. So we have seen that you deepen your knowledge of God through Bible study and finding Him in your Bible, however difficult this may seem at first for a person like me who had never even handled a Bible. Yes, we can do it; we can learn more of God through the book He has chosen to reveal His name and His nature in – the Bible, the 'biblios', the library.

And we have seen that we also deepen our experience as we fellowship with other Christians, especially those who have been Christians for a long time like Tom Fowler, or anybody in a church or fellowship who has had a longer time studying the Bible and waiting upon God than we have had. As I have shared also, I did not find that this was possible amongst the young people at Queen's Hall who were my age and who went to church mainly to please their parents, or better, to mix with friends.

It is essential however, in the Christian life, that we set aside a definite time of day or night when we are going to meet with God, putting everything else away from us and as far as we can from our minds. I would say from my own experience, and the vast experience of other Christians, that a devotional time with God is absolutely essential for a developing Christian life. You will doubtless find as I did, when you set aside this time, there will be many hindrances intruding upon it or calls upon you at that time, but it must be your sacred time, your sacred hour I hope, when you turn aside from all the things that would command your attention in this world of time and space, and things that call for your attention.

Put them aside and get into a solitary place just like Jesus had to do, and meet with God. God has promised, in the epistle of James, 'draw near to God and He will draw near to you,'[45] and Jesus said after the resurrection 'I am with you always, even to the end of the age.'[46] It is not that we have engineered this particular devotion or time to meet with God and He is reluctant to meet with us in any way; it is His desire to meet with us, and I have found that even though I set a time between 5 o'clock and 7 o'clock or between 6 o'clock and 8 o'clock in the morning before things really get going in my mind, for the business of being with God, even then there will be many distractions that will call us away.

My family of four children and my wife had to learn when Dad was having his devotional time that he wasn't to be interrupted, and of course the telephone was always taken off the hook. In my devotional time I didn't usually kneel for my hour or two, I sat in a comfortable chair and for a while just thought about God the best way I could. I loved the words of which the Bible begins, 'In the beginning God made the heavens and the earth.'[47] It is that vast God with whom I am going to meet.

A devotional time, we must realise, is not a one-way conversation of us speaking to God all the time about our cares and concerns and bringing to Him perhaps a shopping list of requests. No, a time with God like this can be spent with nothing ever being said at all. Personally, I think of sentences in the Bible and repeat them, or even verses of a hymn or song and maybe sing them quietly as I think about the being and nature of God, especially about His love shown to the world and me by giving His son to die upon a cross.

When I have, as it were, laid the foundations, or set the course for my devotions, I generally begin to pray, bringing my own needs and requests to God as best I can and knowing that He is hearing. I think about His dealings with me and His promises to be with me at all times. After a while, I begin to pray for other people, those who have asked for my prayers, perhaps they are sick, or those probably who don't know Jesus whom I desperately want for Him to hammer on their heart's doors so that one day they will respond and open their heart's doors and let Jesus in to have fellowship with Him and He with them. So then I may pick up a devotional manual which I am reading, probably one page each day, imbibing and taking in some great Bible teacher or Christian saint's teaching about the Christian life or what to do. God will perhaps speak to me through the Bible verses I have spoken, or through such Christian literature. I pray for missionaries and the wider church of God for some time, and then having simply brought the person to God, not with lots and lots of words, but simply as a person or a cause, just holding it before Him, I begin to listen for Him to speak to me.

I love the words that Samuel said when he was going to hear the voice of God 'Master speak for thy servant heareth,'[48] so I am quiet and listen. Jesus said, as recorded in John's Gospel 'My sheep will hear my voice, they will not follow the voice of strangers; they will recognise my voice.'[49] So I find that God speaks to me in many different ways, very rarely through an audible voice, very often through a vivid and deep impression that He is making on my mind with some promise or instruction that I know is from Him because it's deeply written on my mind and I haven't even been thinking about it. This deep impression on the mind is very important, for God has said in Hebrews 'today if you hear my voice do not harden your heart.'[50] Sometimes He will speak to me through the verse of a hymn or a song. All I know is, the more I listen and take note, the more clearly I hear, and the more time I spend in listening and speaking to God and conversing with Him, the great God of the universe, in a real and meaningful way, the more I deepen my experience with Him.

I like especially to practice meditation, about which I have written a book. People think at first that meditation is simply an eastern discipline of faith, but it isn't. In the Bible it is often mentioned, for instance in Psalm 1, the psalmist says 'upon Thy law do I meditate day and night.'[51] Eastern people, in their false religions, do pray and we don't stop praying because of that; they meditate, yes – we don't stop meditating because of that. It is not whether we or they pray or meditate; it is to whom we pray and about what we pray, and on whom we meditate and what we meditate upon - especially the Bible.

Meditation means that we are very relaxed in body and mind as much as we can ever be, perhaps even lying on a bed. Then we read or bring before us a verse or verses that we have chosen on which to meditate. It is important that we learn the verse or verses by heart, and then we take each word, one at a time; let its meaning imprint on our souls. In Hebrews God says 'the word of God is living and active and sharper than a two-edged sword, piercing to the division of soul and spirit, of joints and marrow'[52]; in Ephesians we read 'the sword of the spirit, which is the word of God.'[53] This means, as we meditate for a long time on a particular verse or passage, it can get right deep within us, deep in our minds, deep in our hearts, deep in our soul, and from there bear fruit in our lives.

So take the verse that says 'Thou wilt keep him in perfect peace; whose mind is stayed on thee, because he trusts in thee,'[54] I make it into this: 'Thou wilt keep me in perfect peace because my mind is stayed on thee, because I trust in thee.' Each piece of that scripture bears fruit in my life because it will penetrate deep in my mind, certainly after a few occasions of using it, and it brings the peace that it promises. Feel the peace, let it roll over you, it is not peace just for this devotional time; it is peace for your day's life and every event in it; you will feel the peace. Psalm 23 is a wonderful passage on which to meditate; learning it and thinking of God as a shepherd, as He is often spoken of in the Bible, and then His provision 'you shall not want'. Picture yourself in the green pastures, by still water, and let the Holy Spirit restore your soul because it may have taken a few knocks the day before. See Him anointing your head with oil; you're an anointed one, a blessed one; your enemies shall not overcome you.

These are just some ideas in meditation and you can get my book 'Meditate and be Made Whole through Jesus Christ' with passages on which to meditate for particular purposes and needs. Eventually, through a prolonged period of life of meditation you will grow, and your fellowship with God will deepen; your knowledge of Him will deepen. I have found meditation to be a habit of life so I don't need to be in a special room or special place; I'll be in the waiting room waiting to see the doctor or the dentist, I'll let my head go back and spend some time in meditation. Especially if I am feeling anxious at any time, I must immediately put myself in, as it were, top gear for meditation, and it will vanish like smoke before the wind.

So a Christian has to practice discipline; a Christian life, especially a devotional life, has to be disciplined. Paul talks about beating his body, bringing it to subjection, bringing it into discipline, so that his soul may be deepened in his experience of God.[55] So don't let anything interfere with your devotional time and if by any chance it has, then find some other time when you can be alone; find even night time on your bed to be alone and enjoy your communion. This prayer is not you talking to God; it is God and you communing; talking to each other.

So we have these practices of Sunday worship with God's people, building each other up in faith, with psalms and hymns and spiritual songs, and teaching maybe from the pulpit and worship. But Christianity is not just a matter of going to church on Sunday morning and that's it, no, that's no way at all to be a Christian. It is living with God all the time, practising being in the presence of God. So you deepen your experience with God, in discussion and sharing with others who know the same faith as you and all the wonders of the being and glory of God, the Father of our Lord Jesus Christ.

PART TWO

Walking with God

through the experiences of life

Chapter 6

Walking with God as companion

We have seen that it is very possible to discover God, not only through our own experience, but because the Bible in fact teaches that God is first of all seeking for us. We are even told that in the Garden of Eden God called out to Adam, who had sinned, 'Adam where are you?' So God desires fellowship with us; He is very close to us. This contradicts very much what John Wesley was himself fighting in the eighteenth century, the theology called 'deism'. This teaching said that there certainly was a God who had created the heavens and the earth but that He had 'wound' the earth sort of like a clock so that it would keep on moving – keep on ticking – and that was all the interest He had in it, and He left it entirely to its own devices, ticking away through the centuries without any interference or even any desire to know what was happening on the part of God. Human beings could not really know Him in any way said the deists, because He is absent.

A similar deist view was expressed many centuries ago by Aristotle who thought that since the heavenly bodies are in motion, they need a mover – an unmoved mover; that God created the world but is just the invisible mover – that's all He ever does, to move the earth on its way. William Shakespeare thought of God as a kind of spectator in the gallery of a theatre with the actors on the stage – human beings playing out their part; a God who had no interest in interfering in any way with what they were doing, but was only an interested spectator. During the eighteenth century deism became popular particularly in the US, England, and France, with the work of philosophers such as John Locke, Voltaire, and Rousseau.

This view of God, as being a creator in a way and absent from any interference or knowledge of the human race, is not what the Bible teaches about God and His relationship to the human race which He in the first instance has created, and in which He has a real interest. We can see that in His coming in Jesus, He interfered, as it were, as we think of the first Christmas, that God became man and was on our level; on our plane. So we see that Jesus, in the New Testament, was how God in fact walked amongst men. Jesus in many places claimed to be not only the Son of God but God Himself. This wonderful news about Jesus Christ is set forth in John's Gospel chapter 1, verses 1-3.

Later, in the Acts of the Apostles, we read of Paul speaking to the philosophers at Athens saying to them, on what was called 'Mars Hill' where they loved to gather every day to hear and learn some new thing, he said to them 'God does not dwell in a temple made with hands, He is not far from any one of us, as your philosophers have said 'in Him we live and move and have our being.'[56]

The New Testament, all the time in its teaching, inspired by God Himself, shows that God not only created Heaven and Earth, but that He remained very close to its natural life and to the human beings that He had first created, and that had gone on generation after generation, still in His interest and in His sight, and with His nearness to every single individual that lives on planet earth.

When Jesus was born, He was called 'Jesus' which means 'Saviour'; He would save His people from their sins. However, in Isaiah, foretelling the coming of the Anointed One, Messiah, He is called Emanuel which, as the Bible says when translated, means 'God with us.'[57] So Jesus was with us, teaching on Earth, we estimate for about three years of our time, and certainly on occasions withdrew to have communion with His Father in secret and in silence. Nevertheless, He was always engaging with human life, often taking the initiative in seeking people like Matthew the tax collector to be His disciple[58]; God calling him as in the story of the Garden of Eden He called Adam.

This amazing truth, spoken of by Paul, and typified in Jesus, shows that indeed God is not restricted to special places like temples or even church buildings. The Roman Catholics hallow their church buildings because they consider them to be the reservation of the 'blessed sacrament' as they call it, the body and blood they believe of Jesus – Jesus Himself. So it is considered a holy place and a place where Roman Catholics will go to find the presence of God in a wonderful way. However, the teaching of the New Testament is quite clear. In John's Gospel, Jesus is found to be talking to a woman of Samaria, not a 'strict Jew', who says to Him 'you Jews say that we should worship God in the Temple in Jerusalem and only there can we really find Him'[59]. Jesus replies saying 'God is spirit, and those who worship Him must worship in spirit and in truth.'[60] Jesus was talking about the coming days, when human beings who are discovering God, as we have seen, then walking with God, can know, indeed by faith, that God is with them at all times and in all places and in all situations.

As we go on in our study, we shall see what difference this presence of God can make. God is very close to a human being who believes, or sometimes one who doesn't believe, because God is taking the initiative to call him and get to know him. By faith he knows that God is with him. Jesus, God incarnate, said in Revelation after His resurrection, in a vision of John the Divine, 'Behold I stand at the door and knock', the door being the human heart, 'anyone that will hear my voice and open the door, I will come in and have fellowship with him and he with me.'[61] This presence of Jesus with us is a marvellous truth as we think what the Old Testament says in Isaiah, God says 'Behold, says the Lord God, the Holy One that inhabits eternity, whose name is holy; though I dwell in a high and holy place I also dwell with him', a human being 'who is of a contrite heart and a humble spirit.'[62] We see that James says, in his epistle, 'draw near to God and He will draw near to you.'[63] Jesus, when addressing the crowds in Matthew's Gospel, says that the Father's knowledge of His children on Earth is as individuals precious to Him; that each individual says Jesus, has hair on his head, which is numbered by God. God knows the number of the hairs on our head; so intimate is His knowledge of us.[64]

We human beings, as I have said of myself until the age of nineteen, live as if we are all that matters in the universe, and that we have to fend for ourselves and make better things of what we have received on planet Earth, for example in medical science overcoming sickness. This is the view of people called 'humanists' today, who believe that human beings are responsible and need always to expect from themselves improvement in their lot of life in every way. They do not believe at all in God and think that human beings are to make their own efforts; every success or improvement is due to human endeavour and God does not in any way promote such well-being that will come to us despite many problems like storms and earthquakes and other natural disasters and bacteria or virus which planet Earth puts on the inhabitants or human beings.

It is possible then, as I have said, to walk through the whole of life as a human being, male or female, for say three-score years and ten, and not sense the presence of God with us at all. So in all situations, like sickness, disease, and facing the finality of death, we human beings struggle on with our own endeavours, trusting in science and technology to make our life better, as indeed in the twenty-first century, compared with the Middle Ages or even the days of the industrial revolution, we have improved the well-being of the human race. It must also be remembered, however, that when we think of progress as a human endeavour, we must remember also that in the twenty-first century human beings have answers that were never dreamed of, more destructive weapons of war that can destroy a whole nation and more destructive weapons in our hands and in our aeroplanes and more terrible means of torturing a fellow human being.

However, if we have made an endeavour to discover God who, as we have seen, is actually seeking us, as the poet Francis Thompson wrote in his poem 'The Hound of Heaven', God is like a hound seeking a fox through many avenues and corridors, corners and niches, never giving up His quest to reach His goal. The Bible does in fact teach that God takes the initiative, sending salvation through Jesus. He doesn't wait for us human beings to act; He is quite capable of doing what He wants to do Himself. So it is sad when human beings are struggling with sickness, like cancers. We feel as though God is unlikely to help in any way and will let us suffer and struggle on until death. However, as we have seen, the Bible teaches that the human experience, like mine over sixty years as an ordinary human being, finds that God in all situations is indeed very close to us as a Heavenly Father who loves us and wishes for our wellbeing. However, He needs us to reach out and grasp His hand to help us. As the Bible says, underneath us are the everlasting arms of God.[65] So maybe in our own bedroom, or in any room in our house, even in hospital, we can find the presence of God very near to us. I, as an ordinary human being, have discovered God amongst His people, that God is very near to each individual person who comprise His people, so that I could in fact discover Him there, and through having times of devotion find even more precious and real, and our help.

So we walk on as the song says 'through the wind and the rain', we walk on but we are never alone. I myself lost my dear wife after fifty-seven years of marriage and eventually found myself a widower in a very nice one-bedroomed apartment, my family mainly living in America because I had taken on a job there as Rector of a church in Seattle and they had come over there to join us and we had to come back because of health to England. So as I survive in the large lounge chair and lovely decorated room all alone, I miss the presence with me of my wife. This is not only in such places as at home but even on our missions overseas where she usually joined me in the ministry of healing. So we had, as it were, a joint ministry, man and wife together, sharing the healing power of God with each other and with those who sought Him, close to them, to heal them, sometimes indeed in the open air, not in a building at all, anywhere, everywhere, there He is ready to hear our cry. So we teach, and I personally testify over sixty years of fellowshipping with God, that He is never absent and I am never alone as I go on through this life to meet, I know, with my wife who is waiting for me in the Heavenly places.

I will just describe one particular occasion when I knew the presence of God with me and this was very, very important and an extremely necessary support of faith. My wife went into hospital to have a polyp removed from her colon. This was to be a simple procedure and I sat in the waiting room for her to have this operation performed as a day patient. The surgeon came out and said 'I've removed the polyp; all is well, come back later and collect your wife to go home'. Believing that all was well, I went and had a meal in a restaurant on the A1 because I hadn't eaten all day. When maybe an hour and a half later I returned to the ward in the Princess Alexandria private hospital where Anne was to be collected by me, I found in fact that all was not well. My wife was critically ill in the operating theatre bleeding to death because the polyp had been so large that the surgeon couldn't remove it, in fact he hadn't even known, because of the quantity of blood coming out, where it actually was in my wife's colon. Apparently he sent for another surgeon to come urgently to help save my wife's life. The surgeon left his home near Stamford and eventually I heard that my wife had stopped bleeding and had been transferred to Room 9.

I was told that she had lost an enormous amount of blood and that her life was in danger and they immediately started to give her a blood transfusion. The room was big enough for me to sit there and watch my wife lie in her bed, very pale and extremely weak. At this time of course, I certainly believed in God. That was a God who was not asleep or watching from the balcony. My wife was in such a terrible state, but He had to be in Room 9 with my wife and with me. I certainly felt His presence in a wonderful way, I knew that He was there through the hours as I stayed there sleeping at night, and over the days my wife in fact recovered her strength and lived her life as a wife and healing minister full of energy.

Of course I thanked the efforts of the surgeons, although they may have been in some way at fault. But I was thankful in my mind because I knew the presence of Almighty God. I did not pray to an unmoved mover, or an eternal clock winder, or a spectator, or any other absentee God. I was conscious that the God and Father, the Lord Jesus Christ was with me and Anne in Room 9.

Chapter 7

Walking with God within you

We have seen in the last chapter, what a wonderful truth it is to know that we can walk with God with us as a companion. Another wonderful truth, surpassing the last one, is that we can walk with God within us. That's the God who created the heavens and the Earth, whom we describe as "almighty, invisible, God only wise, in light inaccessible, hid from our eyes". Also that this great God actually dwells within us is almost incredible but it is true.

Jesus taught this truth to His disciples on the night before He was betrayed. He told them that He would be leaving them but that He would not leave them alone; He would send a comforter or counsellor to be with them.[66] He told them that the comforter would be in them; that He would glorify the Father and the Son; that He would take what belongs to the Son and show it to His disciples.

The word comforter in Greek is 'paraclete'; this is best translated as a helper. The disciples did not know at that time the deep truths about Jesus. For instance, His life became a friend to them at all times; His death became His precious blood, a sacrifice for our sins; His resurrection became His life within our hearts. With the help of the

'Paraclete', Jesus' disciples can know that Jesus is Lord, high above any principalities and powers that ever existed. They learned that this Holy Spirit would overcome their inadequate prayers and take them, with groaning that could not be uttered, to the throne room of God's presence.[67] This truth was taught to the early Christians by Paul and stands as a promise for all time. Christians experience this help today as they pray, walking with God.

The Apostle Paul also experienced the guidance of the Holy Spirit on his missionary journeys. Christians also experience this today. I, myself, pray "May I be in the right place, doing the right thing, for the right reason," every day of my life. So, for instance, I sometimes meet people who I have not planned to meet, and I soon discover why the Holy Spirit wanted me to meet them. I don't call these coincidences, but 'God incidences'. It is wonderful to have this guidance as we walk with God.

We learn from Jesus, in John's Gospel, as he talked to Nicodemus, that the Holy Spirit is active in our new birth, without which we cannot see the Kingdom of God.[68] This is called our 'regeneration'. We are also taught by Paul that the Holy Spirit, God within us, is active for the whole of our Christian life in making us more like Jesus. This is called 'sanctification', being made more holy. As Christians are sanctified, they begin to bear the 'fruits of the Spirit', causing there to be within us love, joy, peace, meekness, patience, kindness, goodness, faithfulness, gentleness and self-control.[69]

God within us, the 'Paraclete', has a definite effect on our bodies and our care of them. The Apostle Paul states that our bodies are temples of the Holy Spirit where God dwells. He says "Do you not know that your body is a temple of the Holy Spirit within you, which you have from God? You are not your own; you were bought with a price. So glorify God in your body."[70]

Jesus taught His disciples after His resurrection "You shall receive power when the Holy Spirit has come upon you; and you shall be my witnesses in Jerusalem and in Judea and Samaria and to the end of the earth."[71] The first disciples received this power on the first Pentecost, described in the Acts of the Apostles chapter 2. They were empowered to fulfil Jesus' command to preach the Gospel to all nations. We are taught in the Bible, and have experienced in our own Christian ministry, that this power is still available for us.

The work of the Holy Spirit, God within us, is as we read in John's Gospel, that everything works to glorify Jesus. He is like the strong light that illuminates, just as a powerful light illuminates an ancient castle set on a hill. We do not look into the light, but at the castle, so the Holy Spirit will not draw attention to Himself, but shines on our wonderful Jesus. The words of a song that describes our sanctification are "Let the beauty of Jesus be seen in me, all His wonderful passion and purity, O thou Spirit divine, all my nature refine, till the beauty of Jesus be seen in me."[72]

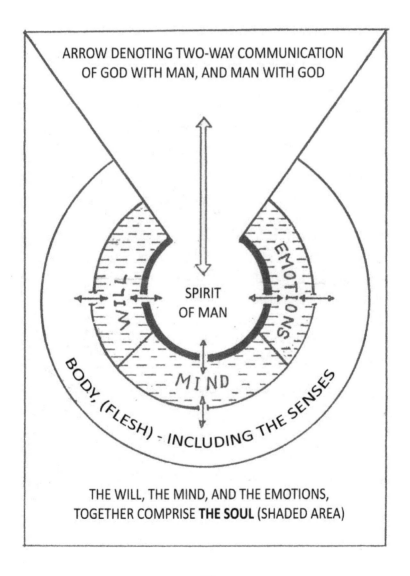

ARROW DENOTING TWO-WAY COMMUNICATION OF GOD WITH MAN, AND MAN WITH GOD

SPIRIT OF MAN

WILL

EMOTIONS

MIND

BODY, (FLESH) - INCLUDING THE SENSES

THE WILL, THE MIND, AND THE EMOTIONS, TOGETHER COMPRISE **THE SOUL** (SHADED AREA)

Chapter 8

Walking with God in marriage and home life

When she was very young, my daughter Rachel said to me, "Dad, I don't want Jesus to come quickly." "Why?" I asked. "Because I want to get married," she said. I suppose it's a desire of most young women and men one day to get married.

In the Bible, however, getting married is not always a desired state for a Christian. Paul actually wrote that it was his desire that people who were Christian should stay in the same state as he was, and he was a life-long unmarried man. However, he also said that Christians should marry rather than burn with emotion. This was, I am certain, because it was thought by Paul that the Lord's return was imminent. He said that a Christian who was unmarried could serve the Lord fully, whereas a married Christian would have divided loyalties.

In the Bible – not in Paul's writing – marriage is regarded as a holy state and a life-long union to which Christians should be called by God. The Church of England prayer book, in its introduction to the Marriage Service says 'Into which Holy Estate these two persons come now to be joined.' The Church of England's Service continues by saying that marriage is primarily called into being by God for the procreation of children. It recognises, however, that not all couples will be granted this joy for specific reasons, for example age or natural causes. It goes on to say that 'Marriage is also encouraged that the natural instincts implanted by God should be hallowed and directed aright.'

The choice of a spouse is one of the most important matters for any Christian to undertake outside his or her decision to be a Christian. In contemporary society, especially in the West, it is considered that the choice of a spouse is about 'feeling in love with a person.' If there is no love involved, the person should not marry that particular man or woman. However, other factors should also be determined, for example the number of children desired by each person, their ages, their religion and faith, their chosen lifestyle and even the influence of family. Those factors will all be important for those who walk with God.

In my life-long ministry, I have been friends with Hindus, whose spouse was chosen for them by parents. I have found that these marriages can endure more than marriages based on so-called 'love'. In modern western society, divorce is often easily embraced rather than a desire to resolve differences. The Church of England prayer book says "Those whom God has joined together let no man put asunder." The impact of divorce by parents can often lead to insecurity among their children, and is the cause of many social and mental health problems in society today.

Christians should better not entertain divorce, and remarriage of divorced people is denounced by Jesus except in Matthew's Gospel where it is said that remarriage can only take place if one of the spouses has committed adultery. With all of this in mind, and a life-long relationship envisaged 'to death do us part', in my case I was married to Anne for fifty-seven years and we have four lovely children. Both of us being dedicated Christians; we walked with God therefore, knowing that everything must be bathed in prayer and God's guidance sought.

In my experience as a pastor, sometimes the fact of forgiveness and the possibility of new beginnings have had a real part to play, especially in the factors of divorce and remarriage. Even a Christian woman being married to a non-Christian husband, is not seen by Paul as a valid reason for divorce. Paul wrote that the husband will be sanctified by the believing wife.[73]

So, walking with God in marriage is seen to be a wonderful adventure of a man and a woman with a family, with Christian teaching from the Bible, and where being members of a Church is seen not just as an added extra but vitally essential to an ideal and wholesome Christian marriage. At marriage interviews, I feel it important to emphasise that each child produced by this couple will be special, and it is essential that each child is brought up as a Christian.

There are some other very important factors in walking with God. It is totally wrong for a Christian to engage in any way in abortion, because in the eyes of God, as is made clear in the Bible, they are committing a murder of a human being, although there may be rare exceptional circumstances. It is also wrong in the eyes of Jesus for a Christian to engage in sexual acts with someone else when their original partner is still alive, unless the other person has already broken the marriage vows. It is certainly wrong for a Christian to commit adultery against their spouse. Even contraception should only be used after mutual agreement as they could be withholding from God a potential child of God. Young children are seen to be especially blessed by God and are to be treated as such in every way. We read in the Gospels that Jesus took young children in His arms and blessed them. He even said that unless adults become like little children, they could not enter the Kingdom of God.[74]

So, the Christian family, husband, wife and children is an entity in itself, and very precious to God. As in all things, pastoral care has to be lovingly applied to all situations. I would recommend that every mother and father, and child if possible, read the last chapters of the first epistle of Peter, and see how this applies. Constant attacks by the devil, and media propaganda, if successful, would destroy the whole of human society. 'The family that prays together stays together.'

Chapter 9

Walking with God at work

I have described my deep devotional life starting usually by about 6 o'clock in the morning every morning of the week. We see that it is easy for a Christian to have such a devotional time and then to close his Bible, get up and close the door of his prayer room, get ready for work and think 'that's my time with God; that's my devotions over, that's the sacred part of my life and now I will go into the secular part of my life and go to work.'

At the time when I came to have my deep experience of God at Queen's Hall in Hull, I was training to be an accountant, a cost-and-works accountant, working during the day at the Yorkshire Electricity Board in Ferensway Hull, then having my tea and going to night school to hear where I left off in my course, training to be an accountant. Such a thought – that my secular life is not related to my Christian life - common as it is, and into which I could easily have fallen into myself, is basically false to the whole teaching of the New Testament about the Christian life. For a Christian, as it is recorded in say the first epistle of Peter, the whole of one's life, even to when you go to bed and say goodnight to the Lord and wake up next morning – all this is sacred; the whole of life is sacred. We cannot at any time turn off, as it were, our

Christianity, or as I am saying – our walking with God, and assume that now that important part of our life is going into some kind of cubby hole or some kind of other part to the main part of our life which is going to work to earn our living. Such work usually means being amongst a lot of other people, male or female, who one is getting to know very well because of the very large chunk of the day that is spent with them, and they are earning their living too, and so we are one in our pursuit, Christian and non-Christian, in our work to earn our living.

As I have said, however, this is a false attitude to the concept of being a Christian and walking with God, because as we enter our office doors with our fellow clerks, we are at that time, and for the rest of the time until we go home, still being a Christian in God. He is walking with us as we sit down to calculate the wages of our employees or fellow workers; God was just as much with me then as He was with me, as I have outlined, early in the morning practicing my devotional life. I was working as a clerk at the Yorkshire Electricity Board in Hull at the time when I had that dramatic experience of God in Queen's Hall on a Sunday night. The next day I went to work, obviously very full in my mind with emotions and with the wonderful encounter I had had with God the night before, and I had to realise that He was now in my work, just as much with me there as He was in the church.

During my time training to be a Christian minister, first in the Methodist Church and then in the Church of England, I had several, as it were, secular jobs. I was a clerk at the Yorkshire Electricity Board, then I went on to be a nursing orderly in various hospitals, also I was a postman at Christmas time, working in the sorting office of a large collection centre, and also I worked as an engineer's labourer. These could be described as my secular employment, but as I have said, as real Christians, we do not make a distinction between the sacred and the secular because all our life, whatever we are doing is sacred.

When I went to work with my new experience deep in my heart and in my mind on that first Monday morning, I was indeed a very changed person. As I sat at my desk, I was conscious that the God who had made Himself known to me the evening before was very much with me at work. I did not of course suddenly stand up in the middle of the office and start to tell my fellow workers that I was now a Christian and start to preach at them, and certainly I would not tell them that in my eyes they were all outside the province of God and in fact unless they too were converted, were going to hell. No, I continued to do my work exactly as I had done it before. I began to talk at break time to my fellow workers and I do not think that they at that time saw a new light shining from my face or a new gleam in my eyes. It was sometime before I had time to tell the man working next to me about my

Christian experience. The subject cropped up in what was to us ordinary conversation. We were asking each other how we had spent the evening before and he was saying he had gone to the cinema to watch a film. With somewhat baited breath I told him something he'd never heard me ever even begin to say before, 'Last evening,' I said 'I was at church worshipping God'. He looked at me amazed and asked me how this change had come about and I began to describe to him my Christian experience.

Work at the office carried on very much as before, but again, through natural every day conversation, I was telling my fellow workers that I had become a Christian. In spare moments we began together to debate what Christianity was about, what it really was in essence. I have to say that I didn't think I had in any way become religious - in the sense of the actual meaning of that word religious. I told them that I had never encountered any kind of Christian service before and that I did not deem myself to have become, as it were, religious which I had always found to be somewhat dowdy and boring to explain. Instead, I told them that in this experience I had found the real meaning and purpose of life.

Eventually, after some months, after talking to the deaconess at Queen's Hall, I began to tell them I was no longer setting out my aim in life to be an accountant, but in fact to become a full-time minister of religion, or rather a full-time worker as a Christian. I eventually told them that I was leaving the office at Yorkshire Electricity Board and going to study the Bible full time at a Bible college in Derbyshire.

It was true that at that time I only had a few pounds in the bank but I understood that at this Bible College you could go free of charge to be taught how to be an evangelist; it was called 'Cliff College' and was in the hills of Derbyshire. I knew now that I had to get some money in the bank, and I saved very hard to provide myself with the necessary books and even utensils for shaving and cleaning my teeth for which I would no longer have any money to rely on from office work, and I worked in my vacations to provide myself with such out-of-pocket expenses.

It was customary at that office of a few hundred workers to have a collection for anybody who was leaving, given out in a meeting after office hours to say goodbye and wish the person well in their new employment. I hadn't really got everything about the Christian faith I wanted to get across to my fellow workers, but they had come to see that I was in some way different, to use Peter's words in the Greek, a peculiar person – a people for His possession[75], and although they couldn't agree with me about believing the Christian faith, nevertheless the collection for me broke all records in the amount given to me in the whole known history of the office. They said that they couldn't understand me as I was doing so well in my training to be an accountant; they even asked if someone had put pressure on me to make these changes and I had to say of course 'no'. But they certainly wished me well and the Director said that if I was ever short of work during vacations I would always be welcome to go back and work a few weeks at the Yorkshire Electricity Board in Hull.

No, I certainly hadn't won any of my fellow workers to believe the Christian faith. They had, however, seen in me they said 'something different' from the normal run of office workers. They certainly had noticed a change in me which I hadn't in any way tried to put on or in any way falsify my whole being. So the so-called secular work had become a sacred means to me for raising money for my Bible college training. Indeed I worked all the time, from that experience in Queen's Hall, not as doing my work at the Yorkshire Electricity Board, but as someone who whilst doing that was really working for God to earn His good pleasure in my office of counting up pounds, shillings and pence. I do not believe that it is a failure if a Christian like me can leave his fellows after several months not having converted one of them to the Christian faith. Most of us in our work, earning our living, are not necessarily evangelists, bringing someone to a full faith in Christ; usually we are 'seed sowers' sowing a bit more of the Christian faith into their lives, or sowing it for the first time that one day may bear fruit at someone else's evangelistic mission. As Paul said 'I planted, Apollos watered but God gave the increase,'[76] for it is only God who can actually work this miracle of new birth or conversion in a human life.

I went on in my five years of study to be a Christian minister to work in several places. Obviously it was quite easy for me to see that I was serving God when dressed in my HMO nurses uniform, or shaving a man, or indeed emptying somebody's bed pan. Yes, nurses can surely see that they are working for God in that employment, but what about being a postman in a sorting office? There I found myself to be working alongside fellow students of my age who were studying for one profession or another, and I found it easy to engage with these young men who were used to discussion; discussing topics, I engaged them in discussion about my intellectual and academic belief in the Christian faith. God was with me; I was walking with God in the wages department of the Yorkshire Electricity Board and again on the hospital wards of the Royal Infirmary in Hull, and again as I was filling mail bags with Christmas presents at the sorting office.

In these occupations I was obviously working with what would commonly be called middle-class men or young men, respectable, good living ordinary citizens. What a shock I had when I started working as an engineer's labourer in the store room of a big factory. I heard a lot of new words, swear words we would call them. I had to listen to a lot of blasphemy as they talked about Jesus and God in a very rude and even profane manner. I did this work for several weeks. Eventually one man asked me 'Are you a student? What are you studying to be or to do?' I said 'I am becoming a Christian minister in the Church of England.' A look of shock or even horror went around on the faces of those men – what had they been saying? What had been their language? What had they said about Jesus Christ? They wished they had known about my goal in life they said. I wasn't sorry that they didn't know because I learned about ordinary men doing an ordinary job in an ordinary place and in an ordinary way, and yes even amongst their profanity I was walking with God and God was walking with me.

I eventually learned that having these so-called 'secular' employments was a really good part of my training for the work I was to do as a Christian minister. I had mixed with ordinary people in ordinary life and it would be to these people I would be addressing my sermons, people like these. I think it is sad when, as many do, people go from high school to university to theological college and into the ministry of the Church without ever really getting to know about ordinary life with ordinary men and women, and what it is like to walk with God and have God walk with you in such situations.

Chapter 10

Walking with God as a single person

As we have seen in a previous chapter, marriage is a special calling of God and not always to be regarded as the state of life for a Christian. I cannot write this chapter with any real authority of my own because I am eighty-seven years of age and I have only been single for a few of them. I do remember however, when I was a young Christian aged twenty, I attended a special evangelical service whilst at Cliff College, having been a Christian for only one year, and there, the particularly captivating preacher, a senior Methodist minister, preached about being a living sacrifice for God. He meant including our pre-conceived ideas about our future. When we are called by God, we are invited to become a living sacrifice for God. When I was called, I know unreservedly that God was speaking to me about my future, including whether or not I would be married. However, I went down the centre aisle of the church and knelt at the communion rail amongst many tears. Soon afterward I met my future wife Anne and we were both committed single Christians.

Instinctively we knew God wanted us to marry each other. We were married for fifty-seven years, until Anne went to Heaven, and produced four lovely Christian children, and knew we were always at the centre of God's will. While sharing our Christian life deeply together, eventually Anne joined me in ministering to sick people as man and wife together. Many Christians told us how wonderful it was to see a man and his wife in joint ministry.

In this chapter, I would regard as a single person, a man or woman, young or older, one who has not been married at all. In the course of world-wide ministry, I have had in my congregations or have met in many other ways, Christians who are single and have had deep fellowship with them. Some have been single from not having met a person with whom, like Anne and me, they have felt the call to marry. Such people I have found have a special calling to serve the Lord in their particular churches. Some have been youth workers or leaders of young people or evangelists and so on, serving Christian vocations in their own churches. Some have had other special calls, for example missionaries and evangelists with such a service that God has established to be filled by a single person.

Paul, in his first letter to the Corinthians, giving advice to Christians, stated that he would prefer all Christians living at that time to remain single like himself. He stated that a single Christian could devote much more time and energy to his or her relationship and ministry for God.[77] A married Christian, he stated, had to give a lot of attention to his or her spouse, whereas a single Christian would be unfettered in this way. So we see that there can be no universal law applied to a Christian as to whether or not he or she should remain unmarried 'for the Lord's sake' or to find mental and spiritual fulfilment in Christian work when such work needs a single person. A definite spiritual decision to remain unfettered by marriage applies to people like monks and nuns who choose to be unfettered by marriage. Those who feel called to the Roman Catholic Church priesthood have definitely made a decision not to marry for life, but as this is a command by their Church, for them I feel that it loses its superiority as a special calling.

Many saintly Christians like Mother Julian of Norwich or St John of the Cross and Mother Teresa of Calcutta in India, have also been single. Bible-believing Christians know that the word 'saint' (Greek 'hagios') is applied to every Christian believer and that every Christian believer has a calling to pursue holiness and this has the purpose of bringing glory to the Lord Jesus to whom they are devoted. This applies to all Disciples of Christ as Jesus told His followers to be 'holy as your Father in Heaven is holy.'[78] This can be through remaining single or through a fulfilled marriage showing love and peace in the Lord. Whether we are married or single, a disciple of Jesus is a light set on a hill for the glory of God.[79]

In the present-day situation, such high and lofty thoughts and ideals are being debased where there is an over emphasis on sexual attraction and sexual activities. Many people prefer not to get married at all but to become 'partners'. Often, it has to be said, such a decision is due to economic factors or causes such as domestic distress at home.

For myself, being a widower living alone did not come easy and needed special regular prayer on my behalf, not to feel lonely but always to feel the presence of God with me. I have now, as a single man, been able to devote a great deal more of my time for my special prayers and devotions than when I was married to Anne. I have also been able to engage in almost unending Christian ministry at all times, so, for example, even yesterday when a young woman suffering from motor neurone disease unexpectedly appeared at the door of my apartment, I was able to give a whole afternoon to ministering to her, setting her free from sin and guilt and bringing to her the peace of God, transforming her in an instant.

So I regard my single life at the moment as a holy calling from God. In all this discussion, we see that a single Christian can fulfil a special calling in God's purposes that a married person would find very difficult. A single Christian is not an island and John Wesley said the Bible knows nothing of solitary Christianity. So a loving Christian church, offering fellowship and friendship, would have both single and married people within its realm and service for the Lord.

Chapter 11

Walking with God through suffering

Human beings suffer since the 'fall of man' in many ways. I have meditated a lot on the sufferings of Jesus, especially on the cross. He obviously suffered agonising physical pain. He also suffered great emotional pain, especially when He cried out "My God, my God, why have Thou forsaken me?"[80] He also suffered at the hands of men by being betrayed by Judas and forsaken by His disciples. He had the additional emotional agony of seeing His mother watching Him dying an agonising death; we can only suffer in the same way although not to the same degree.

If I speak of myself, I have gone through a lot of physical pain and emotional stress, have been persecuted for my faith, and even been forsaken by my relatives and friends. I have met people in terrible pain of all kinds, and have suffered myself enough to empathise with them. In my Christian ministry, or witness to Christ, and seeking to witness and win others for Him, the questions that are repeatedly asked are 'why does God allow good people to suffer?' and 'why is there so much suffering in the world if God is a God of love?'

These questions are difficult to answer, especially when addressing a person who has suffered a great deal. One thing is certain, the world is not as God intended it to be when in the account of Creation it is written "God saw everything He had made, and behold it was very good."[81]

Because of the 'fall of man' recorded in Genesis chapter 3, the human body is decaying, with pain and sickness, and is subject to physical death. We can also say that we have seen in Jesus that God has suffered Himself as much as we do. We can be sure therefore, that God is with us, helping us when we are called to suffer. He does not dwell in a painless unsympathetic eternal domain, but "comforts us in all our afflictions, so that we may be able to comfort those who are in any affliction."[82] He is sympathetic, or more accurately empathetic, in that He suffers with us.

Jesus, God incarnate, went about healing all manner of sickness. In this, He was showing that suffering is not God's perfect will, and all efforts by God and man to alleviate suffering is in accordance with God's perfect will. He has, although He is an almighty God, permitted it because He has given man a free will. The Bible tells us that when Jesus returns in glory, there will be a new Heaven and a new Earth, without any pain or sickness or death, and God will wipe away all tears from our eyes.[83] The Lord's Prayer will be answered, that God's will is done on Earth as it is in Heaven. So we can see that walking with God in suffering gives us the strength to bear it and hope that it will come to an end, for us as individuals and the world itself.

Mental health issues have always been present in human society, but they have become much more recognised, publicised and discussed, especially since Princes Harry and William have made their mental issues public. These issues are much more accepted than they were and treated with an acceptance that it is possible for people from all walks of life, whatever their rank or intelligence, to suffer in this way. It is now thought that at least one in five people will have some kind of mental health issue during their lifetime.

We now ask the question 'what difference will walking with God make to the suffering person?' Jesus Himself taught us not to be anxious about anything in our lives, but to trust God for everything. He reminded us that God clothes and feeds even the least of the birds and flowers, and asked will God not do the same for us.[84] He said "Seek first His kingdom and His righteousness, and all these things shall be yours as well."[85]

Jesus also taught us not to be fearful about anything that might happen to us. He said "Therefore I tell you, do not be anxious about your life, what you shall eat or what you shall drink, nor about your body, what shall you put on. Is not life more than food and the body more than clothing? Look at the birds of the air, they neither sow nor reap nor gather into barns, and yet the heavenly

Father feeds them Are you not of more value than they? And which of you by being anxious can add one cubit to his span of life?"[86]

The Bible itself, and the words of Jesus, are full of words of promise of peace. For instance, Isaiah says "Thou dost keep him in perfect peace, whose mind is stayed on thee, because he trusts in thee."[87] Jesus also said "Peace I leave with you; my peace I give to you. Not as the world gives do I give to you. Let not your hearts be troubled, neither let them be afraid,"[88] and the Apostle Paul writes that Jesus' peace will stand like a sentry before our hearts, saying "The peace of God, which surpasses all understanding, will guard your hearts and your minds in Christ Jesus."[89] All this seems straight forward, and some Christians think therefore that no real believer should ever have mental health problems.

At the beginning of this book, I stated that it was mental health problems that brought me to God, and throughout my life I have been prone to these problems. It has been God Himself who, through His promise, has healed me. So, for nearly seventy years as a Christian, God has kept me mentally healthy. I want to state, however, especially for Christians who have mental health issues and do believe the Bible but nevertheless have continued to have mental health issues, that they should not fear condemnation or guilt, but should continue, despite how they feel, to preserve their belief in God, through which He will bring them to Himself and they will be healed by Him.

I have studied psychology to degree standard, but when I have encountered Christians who have such issues, I begin with the words "If you want a psychiatric answer to your problems then see a secular counsellor, for if you come to me you will get a spiritual diagnosis and a spiritual answer to your needs". I want to say to sufferers that it is much harder to believe the promises of God when you are ill than when you are well. So you may find quotes like "Cast all your anxieties on him, for he cares about you,"[90] and you may really believe this promise and pray, casting each care you have to the Lord, and then find an hour later that the cares have come back again.

I teach in my book 'God and healing of the mind' that sufferers have found that, following the advice in there, that they can be completely healed. I also teach some deep truths in my book 'Meditate and be made whole through Jesus Christ'. I show that there is a difference between simply reading the Bible and its promises, and meditating on them. I teach people to read the Bible and memorise important truths like the ones above and write them down on a piece of card. I also teach how to meditate on each promise for over a week. As we read in the first Psalm "Blessed is the man who walks not in the counsel of the wicked, nor stands in the way of sinners, nor sits in the seat of scoffers; but his delight is in the law of the Lord, and on his law he meditates day and night."[91] This means learning the promise and repeating it continually to get it deep into your mind. We read in Hebrews "For the word of God is living and active, sharper than any two-edged sword, piercing to the division of soul and spirit, of joints and marrow, discerning the thoughts and intentions of the heart."[92]

So, the word you have memorised gets deep within your very being, soul and spirit. It is a living word; it is alive. More alive than any pill you might take; it will do what is says far more than simply reading the Bible. It is through this practice of meditation, for nearly twenty minutes every day, that God has kept me mentally well for so many years.

So do it; take your medication until you are well. Jesus said to one man who had been ill for forty years "Do you want to be well?"[93] If you really do want to be 'well', read the Bible and meditate deeply on its promises, dear reader. You will definitely, if you persevere, be well. So, walk with God, who is very near you and in you, sometimes seeking the help of a Christian counsellor. With regular meditation, you will be well and stay well. All this should become a way of life for you.

Chapter 12

Walking with God through failure

We can all feel a failure at some time in our lives and this applies even when we are walking with God. In fact it can be that through feeling a failure we come to God in the first place and ask for His help. Paul, when expounding the Christian Gospel to the Church of Rome stated that he was once in a condition when he said in some agony "For the good that I will to do, I do not do; but the evil I will not to do, that I practice." and he goes on "O wretched man that I am! Who will deliver me from this body of death?"[94] I am sure that all of us in some way sympathise with Paul, in fact if we want to walk with God in our lives we must realise that we are, in His sight, definite failures.

Paul writes also in his epistles to the Romans that in God's eyes there is none righteous, no not one, "for all have sinned and fall short of the glory of God."[95] That includes you and me also. I want to write about this further by describing my counselling sessions with a lovely, middle-aged, Christian woman. All her life she had been made to feel a failure, firstly by her parents, and then her husband, whom she had divorced. Now, as she was talking to me, she poured out everything in which she had thought she had failed. She was very good at describing her failures. I told her that in the eyes of God she was in fact a failure in her 'natural' life and I sent her away to study her Bible to find out all that she was in fact in Christ. For through her failure she had accepted Jesus as her Saviour from sin, and that was fine, but now she was seeing herself as a failure as a Christian. When she came back for another counselling session and I asked her what she had found out about herself in Christ, she was delighted to say, "I know now that I am not a failure in God's eyes but I am loved by Him unconditionally." This was the first time she had experienced unconditional love and that she had not to earn love by any merit of hers, for it was simply given to her by God, absolutely and unconditionally.

In counselling many Christians like her, I have found that some Christians erect such standards of behaviour and service for God that they cannot possibly attain, and they become so miserable as Christians that I have to say to them that they would have been happier if they had remained atheists. When in the Gospels Jesus speaking through a parable says a steward representing God who has appointed them some tasks does not commend them for any success but, in fact, because they have been faithful.[96] As Christians we have to learn that as we have been saved by God from sin unto life with Him; this was not by merit but by His Grace, "For by Grace you have been saved through faith, and that not of yourselves; it is the gift of God not of works, lest anyone should boast,"[97] so that we have at first been saved by Grace. The word Grace 'karias' means God's undeserved unmerited never ending love. We must trust in God's Grace to keep us going as Christians until by Grace we enter Heaven.

In my own Christian ministry as a clergyman I have sometimes felt an utter failure. When I went to take charge as a vicar of my first parish I found that it was hopelessly divided into different factions. I tried very hard using my natural gifts to heal these divisions. After three years of feeling a failure in this I asked the Bishop to transfer me to another parish which he did. I continued to feel a failure in my ministry until I went to the parish of St. Pauls, in Hainault, when in despair, I asked the Holy Spirit to fill me and completely take over my ministry. After I did this and continued to do this, I saw wonderful miracles of healing by God and thousands of people flocked into my church.

I left this parish in 1979 and have let God take complete charge of my ministry, and it has been wonderfully successful, not by my efforts but by God's amazing Grace. As a sequel to my ministry in my first parish, that I felt I left it as a complete failure, one evening I had an unexpected telephone call from a lady in France. "You will remember me because I was a young person in that parish, and I want to tell you that through your ministry it was completely changed into a community of love. I am telling you this," she said, "because I think you never knew it." In my later ministry I now realise that God not only goes ahead of me into every situation I will face, even in counselling, but that He says He will come behind me; He will " be my rear guard"[98]. In other words whatever I do, if I am trusting in Him alone and am faithful in what I do, He will come behind me in time and place and clear up any mess I have created. What a wonderful God of Grace we serve!

In what I have described as the normal Christian life and service, it is important that we rely on His Grace to be successful. This is an important lesson to learn in every aspect of our Christian life, otherwise, like the lady I counselled, we will feel ourselves to be utter failures, striving always to do better. In my experience in my own life, in the many congregations I have served, I feel that a mature Christian should be a very relaxed person; because he or she is trusting only in God's Grace and therefore cannot fail.

Demos Shakarian in his book writes about the Full Gospel Businessmen's Movement that has swept people into God's Kingdom all over the world, which Demos actually started going with just a few men. He saw that there were far more women in the church than men and started this as a lay-man's movement for men. The concept was that a Christian man should invite an unbeliever to come to a meal with many others like him and that the speaker should not preach a sermon but give his experience as to how he became a Christian. The meeting would include an altar call and healing ministry. He entitled his book "The Happiest People on Earth". That is what Christians ought to be. So if you ever feel a failure in any part of your life, especially as a Christian, take heart in God, as Paul stated that "Yet in all these things we are more than conquerors through Him who loved us."[99]

Chapter 13

Walking with God through the storms of life

"On the same day, when evening had come, He said to them, "Let us cross over to the other side." Now when they had left the multitude, they took Him along in the boat as He was. And other little boats were also with Him. And a great windstorm arose, and the waves beat into the boat, so that it was already filling. But he was in the stern, asleep on a pillow. And they awoke Him and said to Him, "Teacher, do You not care that we are perishing?" Then He arose and said to the sea, "Peace, be still!" And the wind ceased and there was a great calm. But He said to them "Why are you so fearful? How is it that you have no faith?" And they feared exceedingly, and said to one another, "Who can this be, that even the wind and the sea obey Him!"[100]

The above extract from Mark's Gospel is about a sudden and violent storm that arose on the Sea of Galilee. The subsequent account of Jesus stilling the storm is very remarkable but obviously true, especially as it records the disciples' failure to trust Jesus in this situation. I have used this account of the storm to preach a sermon on the 'Storms of Life'. In my vast experience of conversing and counselling with Christians, I have discovered that sometimes their lives seem to be going along in a steady and predictable way, when suddenly, not one thing but lots of events in their lives come upon them all at once, to be paralleled with the sudden onset of storms on the Sea of Galilee. Such events that have happened to them can be sudden bereavement of a loved one, the onset of sicknesses, financial ruin, business failure, panic attacks, and other mental illness problems.

Time and time again such people, devout Christians, even whole families, feel that they are being overwhelmed by these massive and unpredictable onslaughts. They feel that all their securities have gone overboard, like a vessel on the sea, and they are rapidly becoming terrified at being overwhelmed and drowned in all these events. They confess that at such times they, like the disciples on the Sea of Galilee, become terrified and even their strong faith seems to have been of no avail to help them. They, like the disciples, like Peter, cry out aloud or in their hearts 'God don't you care about our situation? Aren't you concerned about what is happening to us,' indeed they think, like the disciples, that their Lord Jesus Christ is asleep and not even awake to their plight.

Why was Jesus content to be fast asleep when His followers were in such trouble? The answer to me is quite plain; Jesus could relax and be absolutely secure in His sleep because, in fact, everything was under control. There was no issue that anything was getting out of hand, because the Sovereign and

Almighty God had charge of every detail of human life and nothing could overwhelm His people; nothing could in any way destroy them because God the Almighty remained on the throne of the universe and its events.

Obviously in this account in Mark's Gospel Jesus had only to speak a word of command for the raging torrents and everything to be absolutely calm and normal. When the storms are at their height it is easy even for mature Christians to doubt God's Providential Care. Jesus scolded His disciples because, having been with Him for some time, they still doubted His ability to protect them from the storms. Before criticising the disciples, we must admit that in the storms of life sometimes our own faith fails.

How frightened or anxious we become will depend not on our faith at that moment but on the faith we have built up in the storehouse of our hearts and minds throughout Bible study, meditation, and prayer, and so we can and should draw on the storehouse of our faith in Jesus at these critical moments. It also depends not on what faith we have at the moment of crisis but on what faith we have built up through our regular, and at times seemingly unimportant, knowledge of Jesus in our lives. Jesus may well criticise us, like the disciples, saying to us, "haven't you got such faith as you should have in me and my authority and power over everything that could happen to you?"

Thankfully, He understands our weaknesses and will always bring us through to a place of calm, rest, and peace, for which we will forever thank Him, and see that "human extremity is God's opportunity to act for His people."[101]

I have certainly experienced such times of storms and subsequent wonderful peace in my long Christian life and ministry. Because I have engaged very boldly and powerfully in Spiritual Warfare, the enemy, or the devil and his angels, have launched sudden attacks on me and even on my family. At one time under such attack I felt I was being strangled to death in my own bedroom and I praise the Lord that many Christians, realising my bravery in casting out many demons and the likelihood of terrible counter attack from the occult realm, have prayed for me. I am thankful to be able to testify that after sixty-seven years as a Christian, He has always brought me through such attacks and frequent storm-like events in my life, so that as I write I am in a place of tranquillity and calm.

So I have used this simple, yet graphic, story given to us by the Holy Spirit to encourage and help many Christians as they walk with God through the storms of life. Without such walking with God, if they were simply people of unbelief of the Word and with no real concept of God's power, they would definitely go under the waves, and sadly, I have seen many metaphorically drown. So let us again take hold of our journey through life with God, whether on land or sea, and claim the victory, even when our Lord has seemed to be asleep. Let us transpose into this teaching the old hymn "Eternal Father, strong to save, whose arm does bind the restless wave, Who bids the mighty ocean deep its own appointed limits keep; O hear us when we cry to Thee for those in peril on the sea."[102] Of course we mean the sea of life.

Chapter 14

Walking with God as a senior citizen

The age at which we can be described as a 'senior citizen' varies very much in contemporary thought. Usually it is taken to be the age when we receive our state pension, say at sixty-five years of age. However, many people are still very active and agile at this age and do not regard themselves as senior citizens. In my own case, now aged eighty-seven, I still remember not regarding myself as a senior citizen even at the age of eighty. Since that time, certain conditions have taken hold of me, described by the medical profession as age related, such as losing my eyesight (macular degeneration) and arthritis that has affected my ability even to walk. Many people have these and other conditions of old age afflicting them, though some people are still very fit in their late nineties. Such things as Alzheimer's disease and the deterioration in their brain cells affect their memory. Thankfully, my brain and memory are crystal clear as I write this book. How then does a person walking with God think and react as a senior citizen?

Paul, in his letter to the Philippians, which I certainly did not like as a young man, advised the Christians saying "Brethren, I do not count myself to have apprehended; but one thing I do, forgetting

101

those things which are behind and reaching forward to those things which are ahead, I press toward the goal for the prize of the upward call of God in Christ Jesus."[103] Surely, as senior citizens we can look back on certain events in our life with gladness because, for example, Jesus has stilled the storms of life for them, and this gives them encouragement for the future. I think what Paul is saying is that we must not 'live' in the past, but face the present time with its anxieties and problems with the real faith we have now at this time.

Living in the past can be a real hindrance at times to spiritual progress. Paul is also saying that we must always have a positive aspect to our lives and look to our future service for God and His blessing. Certainly, when in older age, Christian people do have more time to spare for the things of God, although such things as child minding for their now older and married children must also be seen as a Christian service. Often in older age Christians have faced bereavement in the passing of much loved friends or relatives and so must have a positive attitude towards life after death. I myself lost my wife at the age of eighty-two and was tempted to retire from Christian ministry and just live in the past of my happy married life and much blessed service for the Lord. I had, in fact, retired in this way when a younger Christian woman, named Elizabeth Young, challenged me in a phone call by saying "Can you remember in the Bible anyone who retired from service to God? "Trevor", she added, "the anointing of God is still upon you, rise up and start ministering once again." I have done this and had a wonderful ministry, even to setting a clergyman free from the power of the occult and Satan. Probably I was one of the few people in England who could accomplish this for him, through my spiritual discernment and uncompromising belief in the power of the Name of Jesus. So as Paul commanded, I still press on in service in the future.

I must write a few things about bereavement as I have faced this also. I have noted that most of the well-known Christian hymns always have a verse to end with looking forward to the joy and glories of heaven. So for instance, Charles Wesley's hymn "And can it be" ends with "Bold I approach the eternal throne and claim the crown through Christ my own."[104] I have dwelt a lot on my bereavement, and to my ever-approaching passing, on such hymns, for example the magnificent hymn of victory by Paul in 1 Corinthians "For this corruptible must put on incorruption, and this mortal must put on immortality. So when this corruptible has put on incorruption, and this mortal has put on immortality, then shall be brought to pass the saying that is written: 'Death is swallowed up in victory. O death where is your sting? O Hades where is your victory?'"[105] Also in 2 Corinthians "For we know that if our earthly house, *this* tent, is destroyed, we have a building from God, a house not made with hands, eternal in the heavens."[106] So, senior citizenship for a Christian need not be a weak and morbid life, but one full of hope and joy as they dwell in the Lord and the Lord in them.

PART THREE

Serving God

Chapter 15

Serving God as a bond servant

It is an age old maxim to say 'we are saved to serve.' I don't think this is always true, as 'being saved' is an end in itself without anything further being added to it, for we are then in glorious communion with God through the merits and death of our Lord Jesus Christ. When I was saved at the age of nineteen, I immediately wanted to be of service to help bring in further, in my little way, the Kingdom of God. I have described all of this calling in my companion book entitled 'Divine Healing, Deliverance, and the Kingdom of God'.

I have quoted the Apostle Paul a lot in my description of the Christian life, and certainly when the Lord Jesus appeared to him in a light "brighter than the sun,"[107] Paul was immediately called to serve the Lord, which he did as the first missionary of the early church, travelling all over the Roman Empire as it was at that time. I like to illustrate why he was such a servant of the Lord Jesus using a story I heard of a woman, in the days of the slave trade, who was much desired by slave masters. On being sold at a slave market, the price paid for her by one man was extremely high. As this woman went to her new owner she said to him "I hate you,

I loathe you; I will only serve you with resentment in my heart." The man who had bought her said to her "You have it wrong; I paid that price for you with all the money I have in order to set you completely free." "Sir," she said, kneeling before him, "I will serve you forever."

The Lord Jesus Christ, in fact, paid the ultimate price of giving His life as a sacrifice to God to set us free. When Paul heard the Lord Jesus, as he was going on the Damascus Road to persecute Christians and put some to death, and knowing that, having incriminating documents upon him, and with no excuse at all to give to the Lord Jesus, He, The Lord Jesus, had appeared to him to set him free of all guilt. In his heart he said 'I will serve you forever.'

Paul began, as it is written in the Greek, describing himself as the bond servant of the Lord Jesus. The word 'bond servant' literally means a slave by his own will and determination. Being a slave meant, in fact, that his hours of service would be unlimited, as we would say 24/7. As a willing slave, his service would know no set hours, no reward, and no conditions. After my own coming to know the Lord Jesus, I too wanted to serve Him as a 'bond servant.' I gave myself to Jesus in a limitless way and have served him unstintingly to the present time.

It is true to say of any person who gives themselves in full-time service to the Lord Jesus Christ, in whatever He calls them to do, they become Jesus' bond servant like Paul. So, for instance, when I became a full-time ordained minister, I was told I would not receive any salary as such, or so much per hour, per day or per week. Instead, I did receive what is called a stipend; this meant an allowance that the church thought was needed for me to be able to serve and support a wife and four children. The same has been true to this day, especially when I began to live by faith in 1979. I didn't even receive a stipend or any fixed allowance from anyone as I was an evangelist, an itinerant one, to every nation where I was called to go. So I describe myself as a world-wide itinerant evangelist, preaching the Gospel, healing the sick, casting out demons; a ministry I still undertake today, relying solely on what any church gives me or any person does, to this present time.

I must say in all these years, I have never been in want for what I needed to live on. I cannot say, like John Wesley "I have somehow become rich". I have never charged anyone in any way for any ministry I have undertaken to them as individuals or a church. I have taken as my motto the Bible words of Jesus "Freely, freely you have received, freely, freely give."[108] I describe the terms on which I live like the Apostle Paul as a "bond servant of God and an apostle of Jesus Christ."[109]

As I look back I have lived a wonderful life; it has been a tremendous adventure and I just hope when I pass from this world, by the Grace of God, and not by any merit, I will hear Him say "Well done thou good and faithful servant." My children, who are all Christians, say, "Dad it will take you a very long time to get into Heaven pushing through the crowd that will be waiting to greet you." Such is the life of myself and thousands of others who, having realised Jesus has paid the price to set them free of all guilt before a Holy God, have said in their hearts to Jesus "Lord, I will serve you forever."

Chapter 16

Serving God in worship

The word 'worship', means in the Latin, to 'ascribe worth'. In our Christian faith, this means to ascribe absolute worth to the God and Father of our Lord Jesus Christ. The first commandment given to Moses, in the list of the Ten Commandments, and repeated by Jesus in Luke's Gospel says "Thou shalt worship the Lord Thy God and Him only shalt thou serve."[110] Very few Christians realise that worshipping God is the greatest act of service they can render to Him. Probably, it is true to say that human beings alone in creation can worship God in communicating with Him. Acts of worship are a two-way matter. Objective worship means that we are concentrating solely on God Himself and addressing Him alone, by the attitude of our hearts and the words of our lips. It is obvious that such acts of worship are typically rendered once a week in church services by faithful Christians. They try to turn their whole being towards God and address Him in hymns that are usually majestic such as:

> "O worship the King all-glorious above,
> O gratefully sing of His power and His love;
> our shield and defender, the Ancient of Days,
> pavilioned in splendour and girded with praise."[111]

This worship to God is helped by some, including my late wife Anne, by the building they are in. She liked to be surrounded by wooden pews; all facing what she called the altar. She, and many others, are also helped by the presence of stained glass windows and marble arches. On the other hand some Christians prefer a much more informal setting for worship, for instance simply having individual chairs in a sort of school hall environment, facing the pulpit or rostrum, where the leader of the worship has placed him or herself. They would also go along with Paul's exhortation in Ephesians to "Be filled with the Spirit, speaking to one another in psalms and hymns and spiritual songs, making melody in your hearts to the Lord."[112] They usually prefer to sing to God, not in verses of hymns accompanied by an organ, but in simple songs often called 'choruses' that express the love they feel for God and the freedom they have to worship Him in their hearts:

> "I love you Lord, and I lift my voice
> To worship You O my soul rejoice.
> Take joy, my King in what you hear,
> Let it be a sweet, sweet sound
> in Your ear."[113]

For many Christians the most ultimate and highest form of worship is what Roman Catholics call The Mass or the Church of England's worship called the Eucharist. This takes a liturgical form of worship leading towards the taking of bread and wine in obedience to what Paul called the Lord's Supper, set out by him in his letter to the Corinthians "For I received from the Lord that which I also delivered to you: that the Lord Jesus on the same night in which He was betrayed took bread; and when He had given thanks, He broke it and said, "Take, eat; this is My body which is broken for you; do this in remembrance of Me." In the same manner He also took the cup after supper, saying, "This cup is the new covenant in My blood. This do, as often as you drink it, in remembrance of Me," For as often as you eat this bread and drink this cup, you proclaim the Lord's death till He comes."[114] Whatever form, either the liturgical or extemporary, nearly all Christians regard this act of worship a very solemn occasion deserving the confessions of their sins and the rededication to the Lord of their lives.

An American University, some time ago, in a survey of Christians going to church to worship, whether in a solemn building or school hall, found that especially with the solemn building called a 'church' the worshipers approached from afar in a relaxed and happy manner, but as they approached the church they became very solemn and seemed even sad. They noted that the worship, especially of a liturgical type, was also very solemn and the worshipers even left the church in a solemn mood, but when they moved further away from the church building they became relaxed and happy again. This certainly goes along with the common idea that worship in church must be serious and solemn. Such worship attitudes have been diminishing and the more relaxed and joyous way of worship, often with singing of choruses for a long period of time, is quite rapidly increasing in the number of peoples who worship in this happy and joyous format.

I refer again to the fact that whatever the manner, and wherever the place, in which Christians worship, we should be ascribing absolute worth to our Creator and Saviour God. What I wish to point out however, is that in New Testament teaching, worship for Christians, which in the early days was usually in the homes of believers, should not be a once-for-all act once a week, but a continued attitude of mind and heart of a loving attitude to God in the whole of their conscious lives. This involves, of course, the worship of God in our own personal or family devotions and even in our spiritual conversation. The constant theme in our thoughts should be:

> "Great Father of Glory, pure Father of Light
> Thine angels adore Thee, all veiling their sight; All laud we would render, O help us to see: 'Tis only the splendour of light hideth Thee."[115]

So as we see, the worship of God is a most wonderful and happy service that Christians can offer in daily response to His unfailing love. The more joyous sort of worship that I have described is not usually accompanied by an organ playing the tune but often by a miniature orchestra comprising especially guitars and drums and the keyboard which aids this type of worship much more than the solemn tones of an organ. Worship in other settings is often accompanied by the reading of Holy Scripture; the Old Testament and especially The New Testament are used in liturgical worship and a reading of the Gospels of the life and ministry of our Lord Jesus Christ is always included. A passage is often read on which the minister or pastor intends to elaborate by the preaching of what is often called a 'sermon' in which the preacher intends to edify, instruct, encourage, teach, and sometimes even challenge, his Christian listeners.

The aim of all this objective worship has a definite subjective effect on those who are worshiping. It refocuses their lives from their everyday existence in the secular world, on to what really matters to them most of all, our spiritual life of the Kingdom of God. Whatever, and however, the manner of worship, whether in a public setting, or in personal thanksgiving and love, it will, in fact, if rightly and sincerely offered to God, draw the worshipper into a deeper relationship and communion with God, and have a subjective effect of giving a deeper communion with the Father of our Lord Jesus Christ. Ideally, it will draw the worshipper right, as it were, into the heart of God in the words I love to quote:

"There is a place of quiet rest, near to the heart of God, a place where sin cannot molest, near to the heart of God.
O Jesus, blessed Redeemer, sent from the heart of God, hold us, who wait before thee, near to the heart of God."[116]

In my own devotions in the worship of God, sometimes I am drawn to that place which is beyond words or explanation, where one rises from worship and one knows where they have been, in the Spirit, in deep communication with the Creator of the ends of the earth. In all this, Christians must worship God as Jesus taught in John's Gospel "in spirit and in truth"[117] for in such a way God wishes them worship Him. Obviously anyone who is walking with God and serving Him will put worshiping God as the highest and most important factor in their spiritual life. This applies to private devotional life and corporate 'church life' and worship with fellow Christians.

Chapter 17

Serving God in ministry

The Apostle Paul, in his letters in the New Testament, discusses several areas of service, for the worshipping church that he calls "the body of Christ."[118] This image denotes how, in their life together, Christians are as close to each other as any organ of the body can be to the building up of the whole. In fact the Greek word 'melos', translated as members, means a bodily organ or limb; the working parts of a body or machine; like members of a sports team. So Paul is talking about Christians not just being close together but in fact sharing lives as though they are the working parts of the same body or instrument where all the parts matter.

In this sort of 'church', the word translated as 'church' from the Greek 'ekklesia' never meant a building or an institution, but rather an assembly of, as I have previously stated, 'the called out ones'. In others words denoting a set of people not an edifice of any kind. In this 'body', Paul teaches in his letter to the Ephesians that certain areas of ministry will in fact arise, given to the church by the Holy Spirit. These ministries are named as: apostles, prophets, evangelists, pastors and teachers, with the latter implying in the Greek one ministry and not two, so that the pastors are also called into being by God, as teachers to address and exhort the Christian congregation.[119]

Whatever the calling however, Paul expects these to grow out of the body of the church, through the action of the Holy Spirit. It is important in the life of a congregation for Christians of any denomination in the church today, that such ministers of the Gospel do not set about 'doing their own thing'. In the teaching of the New Testament, when such ministries are called into being, they are seen to be so called by God to the whole congregation in which they are to serve. In my own spirit-endowed churches, the elders of the church (described this way in Paul's letters to Timothy and Titus) together recognise that the minister has been called by God to officiate and they often lay hands on him or her in the presence of the congregation to confirm that this particular person has been recognised in their ministry by the elders; blessed by them and so the congregation can receive them with real authority; answerable to the elders for what they actually do in the congregation. This, in today's churches is readily recognised as a proper way to acknowledge and authorise pastors and teachers.

The ministry of prophets, I have found in my travels around the world, to be rather scarce. However, in my own spirit-filled congregation at St Paul's, Hainault, we did recognise the ministry of prophets because prophecies as such were frequent utterances in the church. To recognise a prophet scripturally is seen in that if they are forth-telling the future, so what they prophecy actually comes to pass. However, prophecy is not always related to future events that are often on a national scale, but for a congregation, and given during worship; they are sharing with the believers something about the mind of God himself. I was not only recognised in my church as a pastor and teacher, but also as a prophet declaring, often in poetic language or picture language, some spirit-filled message that God wished to teach my congregation.

In my teaching on this subject I do not believe a prophetic utterance could be preceded by 'Thus says the Lord' as if it were as infallible as the Bible, but rather begin with such words as 'I believe the Lord is saying'. Paul teaches in his letters that such utterances must be weighed by either prophets or the elders as being true, and in fact they would never, in any utterance, in any way, contradict what God has said once for all in the Bible. So, for instance, when a man uttered the words "I believe God is saying that I should leave my wife and get attached to my spiritual mistress," we immediately recognised this as contradicting Biblical teaching and had to describe the man as a 'false prophet'. Where, however, ministries named by Paul in Ephesians truly come into being through the action of the spirit of God, the church in question is very enriched, often exhorted to deeper life with God and often ejected into rapid growth in numbers by the hand of God. I remember once, a man - quite a new Christian - who had been recognised by the leaders as a prophet, shared with the body of Christ at Hainault; he saw in a picture a tree with its branches spreading far and wide but with its roots in very shallow ground. We recognised that he was speaking of our own church with its message having spread all over England and indeed to many parts of the world as these far reaching branches denoted, but we know that through this prophet the Lord was telling us not just to concentrate on spreading the word further afield, but as a church to concentrate on our inner life, going deeper into the life of the Spirit and of God himself; to deepen our roots.

Such lessons were constantly being ministered to us in the Spirit, often to our surprise, but always to our delight and joy in the Lord. Paul, in his first letter to the Corinthians, indicates that the Holy Spirit would give special supernatural gifts to Christians in a congregation according to His will. These gifts are named by Paul in his letter to the Corinthians as: wisdom, word of knowledge, faith, healing, miracles, prophecy, discerning of spirits, tongues and interpretation of tongues.[120] It is to be noted that these gifts are supernatural endowments by the Holy Spirit and usually not in any way consistent with a person's natural abilities in the church or secular world. Thus for instance 'the word of knowledge' in this chapter does not indicate the ministry of a Christian, who for instance had been to university and studied theology, or any other natural study. It denotes rather a person being given by the Holy Spirit 'supernatural knowledge' that he would not know in any way by him or herself in secular study.

In the life of our Lord Jesus, who was in fact endowed with all these supernatural gifts, He used the word of knowledge when he said to a woman at Jacob's well, recorded in John's Gospel "You truly said you had no husband, for you have had five husbands and the man you are with now is not your husband."[121] This utterance of supernatural knowledge of this woman caused her to say to her friends, "Come and see a man who has told me everything I ever did."[122] This in fact resulted in many people in her town believing in the Lord Jesus Christ as Messiah. On another occasion Jesus used a word of wisdom when speaking to the Pharisees who thought that they had asked Him an unanswerable question about what taxes they should give to Caesar. Jesus replied with the words of wisdom, "Render to Caesar the things that are Caesar's and to God the things that are God's."[123] The scripture then says, after that answer no one dared ask Him any more questions. It is recorded in the Old Testament that God supernaturally endowed King Solomon with such incredible wisdom that people, Kings and Queens, including the Queen of Sheba, came from lands afar to hear the Wisdom of Solomon.[124]

I am amazed at the misunderstanding in modern Bibles of the gift of 'tongues'. It is often translated as 'the gift of foreign languages'. It may be thus, as on the Day of Pentecost, when people from all over the Roman Empire heard the apostles speaking in their own particular languages which the hearers knew they could not have possibly learned, but Paul teaches that this gift of 'tongues' can either be in the language of men or indeed of angels, and it needs a supernatural interpretation which he says should always come, an utterance in tongues, not to translate it but to interpret its meaning for the hearers. It seems that in Corinth utterances and the use of the supernatural gifts denoted by Paul had become chaotic, and in his letter, Paul denotes definite rules which the Corinthian church must use for these supernatural gifts.[125] Paul states that the Holy Spirit is the author of peace and order and not in any way of confusion.

The emphasis on spiritual gifts, or in the Greek 'charisms', was seemingly rediscovered and widely used in what has been called the Charismatic Movement throughout the world or the Christian church in the 1960s to the beginning of the 21st century. Christians gathered in very large numbers to hear this seemingly massive invasion of the Holy Spirit into the church's life. Especially used was the gift of healing as denoted by Paul, resulting in many unusual and almost incredible miracles, in which I myself was so used by the Holy Spirit in the life of my church St. Paul's in Hainault, Essex, that thousands of people with illnesses and afflictions came from all over England and the world for their special miracles. It is sad that much of this has died out in the life of the Christian church as Christians pray, 'Revive our church Lord, as they look again for a miraculous out-pouring of the Holy Spirit which alone will keep the church of God alive and spread its message throughout all the world.

Obviously, a Christian walking with God will be praying by him or herself and, joining with other Christians in prayer for revival inspired by the Holy Spirit to happen quickly. The Christian knows that such a movement of the Holy Spirit puts into pale perspective even sincere efforts by the church to organise outreach and missions. Again, a Christian walking with God will ask the Lord to give him or her effective ministry in the church, especially to edify other Christians, and will seek, as Paul says they should, the higher gifts rather than that they should prophecy;[126] he or she will want to be a really effective spirit-filled minister to build up the body of Christ.

Chapter 18

Serving God in spiritual warfare

The need for teaching on this subject came forcibly home to me just yesterday, when I was counselling and ministering to a very sincere and devout Church of England clergyman, who eventually agreed with me, that teaching on spiritual warfare was almost totally omitted from the teaching of the church, and in particular its preparation for service in key Christian ministries, such as being a vicar of a Christian congregation. I remember myself as a young Christian at Bible College, walking down a country road with a friend and saying, "I don't believe in the devil; evil solely resides in the hearts of human beings, and they should not blame a devil for their own evil or wickedness in the world." My friend reported my lack of belief in the devil to the Principal of the college, as this was considered to be very serious. The Principal summoned me for a special time with him in his study and lent me books on this subject, for instance 'The Screwtape Letters' by C.S Lewis which taught in graphic form the reality of Satan, through his devils, planning to destroy Christian congregations. For C.S. Lewis, a very learned Christian Professor, evil was not only a powerful force but also had a mind that could think and plan its exploits. I became somewhat convinced of the reality of the devil through this and other books.

I have described in my companion volume 'Divine Healing, Deliverance and the Kingdom of God', how in 1970 I was pushed into spiritual warfare at great depth by God Himself, when a witch tried to strangle me, and I had to cast out evil spirits from her life. She became a wonderful Christian member of our congregation. After this event, I was engaged in spiritual warfare, describing on national television the terrible decline of morals in Britain's 'permissive society', stating publicly "The devil is behind this lot". I was so involved, even on nationwide television, in spiritual warfare that I became dubbed 'the exorcist vicar', and in one of my books called 'Supernatural Superpowers', on the cover it said "England's Exorcist writes about Supernatural Superpowers." Once, in driving into the town of Burnley, there was such publicity, when I myself dared to undertake a Christian mission to the town, that on most of the lamp posts in the streets there were placards stating "Exorcist Arrives in Town." So, with many years of engaging in spiritual warfare (the word exorcist is a spiritualist label for Christian deliverance ministry), I was, therefore, well equipped to speak to this Church of England vicar, and to Christian churches in general, about spiritual warfare.

I have learned, both from scripture and my own very wide experience, that Satan is alive and active, and very powerful indeed in the world today, often even getting hold of sincere Christians for him to use for his purposes. In the New Testament Peter warns in his letters that Christians should, "Beware, because the devil goes about as a roaring lion seeking whom he may devour."[127] Paul teaches in Ephesians that, "We wrestle not against flesh and blood but against principalities and powers and world rulers of wickedness in high places."[128] He urges Christians to put on what he calls, "The whole armour of God"[129] to protect themselves from these powerful evil spiritual forces.

In my experience of spiritual warfare, I have seen that Satan's kingdom is really what we would call 'the occult' dimension of spirituality. Biblically, this is shown in the Acts of the Apostles when Paul and Silas on their missionary journeys, entered a very high Roman official's house and found that his whole household had been what he described as "bewitched" by a certain man named Elymas the sorcerer.[130] Paul, to demonstrate that the power of the Holy Spirit was stronger than anything Elymas could produce, struck the sorcerer blind. Elymas cried out for mercy, received his sight and he and the whole household of Sergius Paulus became Christians.[131] On another occasion Paul and Silas entered a town called Ephesus and met a slave girl with an infallible ability to tell fortunes for which her owners received much money.[132] Paul cast a spirit out of her, an occult spirit, and she was no longer able to ply her trade. The narrative goes on to say that when her masters saw that their hope of gain had gone they stirred up a whole rabble of people in that city to persecute Paul and Silas.[133]

These sorts of things are not make believe, for I have had to cast out spirits from young people who are in a dreadful state mentally and spiritually through having their fortunes told by a gypsy in Stamford Market. I recently met the Master of a pleasure liner who was in charge of a huge pleasure boat with hundreds of passengers going on round-the-world trips, and who, before one such trip, learned that the owners of the boat had engaged a fortune teller to be on board in the capacity of an entertainer. This Master, who walked with God, knew that this was not just entertainment but a very powerful and dangerous energy for all who went to see her to have their fortunes told. He told the owners of this boat that he would give up his job as the Master of the ship (which would have cost him his job and the loss of many thousands of pounds in income) unless they told this woman she would not be employed by them. This took great courage for him but he got his way, the Lord Jesus was glorified, and all went well.

In my experience it is such entanglements with seemingly mundane and harmless pursuits, that in fact, permit the invasion of powerful spiritual forces of evil which Satan uses to trap unwary people. In one incident some years ago I was called by a Christian Headmaster to a school where four senior pupils had decided to spend their free time playing about with an Ouija board. They thought it was harmless but went into trances and one was about to kill a fellow pupil apparently on the instigation of his dead grandfather. Thankfully I was able to set these pupils free and they did not ever play about with occult things again.

Returning again to my counselling and subsequent ministry to the Church of England vicar, his troubles began when he was asked to go to a country in the Far East that turned out to be a country where Christianity was hardly known and occultism ran rife. He had not been taught about any of the dangers of being involved in occult practices and he went there in all innocence. It was a woman he did not know, and whose presence he did not in any way seek, who suddenly accosted him and without being asked, told him of all the events in his past life. He was amazed because she could not have known any of these things in any natural way. She then said to him, "I have told you about your past and when I meet you again I will tell you everything about your future." Thankfully, he avoided her in the future, but this was when the troubles in his life and family began in an amazing way which took him nearly two hours to relate to me.

These events were, by any normal standard, extraordinary, involving so-called religious objects, even one person being incited to commit murder which he did, and some very strange illnesses that could not be medically diagnosed affecting his person and family. The incidences included strange meetings with his daughters being involved in a store room with a woman, who was found in fact, not to exist, and so the story went on of supernatural (not Christian) events that he had related to others. I think they thought he was just fantasizing, but when he told me of them I recognised each one as having occurred sometime in my ministry of spiritual warfare. He said at the end that everything in his life had gone wrong, his financial situation had become desperate, no one had believed his story and he was at his wits end as to who to turn to and where to go. It was not by chance but by the Lord's leading that he was directed to me, a clergyman whom he did not know. It was not the first time the Lord had brought to me someone in such a predicament, so I was able to say I believed everything he had told me, and in my laying of hands on him he was set free from all the terrible occult bondage in which he had unwittingly been trapped.

On a subsequent visit to me he said "Pastor, in my ministry I felt full of the Holy Spirit", an experience that he had never had since going to that church in the Far East. I feel therefore, that I had to write this chapter to warn those who are walking with God and even seeking supernatural power to be very careful indeed and not get involved in any way with anything that is spiritualistic, paranormal or of non-

Christian origin, however attractive such an incursion may seem.

The Lord has used me very powerfully and dramatically in this ministry of deliverance which I describe in my companion book. I did not want this ministry and I did not like this ministry and would have avoided it if I could. I wanted to engage solely in a ministry of evangelism and divine healing, but the Lord Himself has, as it were, piled this ministry upon me. I have seen the power of the Name of Jesus and His supreme authority over all satanic occult forces that I, in the ministry of obedience, have had to engage with, even when threatened with death on a card written in blood by a spiritualist.

In particularly, I have got into problems when stating that homosexual and lesbian practices are from the evil one. I am sure the people whose sexuality can thus be described are not in themselves evil in any way. Certainly such as I have met, and spiritualists I have met are usually very kind, gentle and lovely people, some even have a sincere Christian faith. It is not the perpetrators described by Paul in his letter to the Romans, who are in any way evil, but what they practice. Paul, in his letter to the Romans makes this clear, saying that "For even their women exchanged the natural use for what is against nature. Likewise also the men, leaving the natural use of the woman, burned in their lust for one another, men with men, committing what is shameful, and receiving in themselves the penalty of their error which was due."[134] Not only this but other statements in the New Testament describe such acts as evil. I have said in sermons that the power and authority of the name of Jesus is able to set any person in such a situation entirely free from their entanglements.

The New Testament in fact, only speaks of Satan and his minions and works in the same sentence as declaring the complete victory of Jesus over them. So Paul states that Jesus "is far above all authority and power that can be named in this world and the next."[135] It is very sad that I have seen, even very recently, a meeting where a medium would try to get in touch with so-called dead people, to be absolutely packed with people, even paying £10 to be admitted, when a Christian ministry of healing could only attract a handful of believers. There is an account of seeking a medium to contact the dead in the Old Testament. King Saul sought out a woman known as 'the witch of Endor'[136] to tell him how a battle the next day would transpire for him. In this account it is stated that the dead prophet Samuel appeared and said, "Why have you brought me up?" and continued "tomorrow you and your sons shall be with me."[137] On the next day King Saul was killed in battle.

I want to say that with the seeming dearth of powerful New Testament teaching, occult practices can seem attractive to the unwary person. It is incumbent on those who are walking with God in service to Him, to avoid all contact with the occult, warn people of the dangers, even such as dressing up as witches at Halloween, engaging in role play games such as 'Demons and Dragons', reading books that contain stories of magicians, however fictitious they may seem. Even watching such things in films or on television can be very spiritually harmful. So those walking with God will also learn how to set free those with whom they meet who are in distress through occult involvement. I am eighty-seven years of age, still engaged in this ministry as I walk with God, and I find it very exacting and very exhausting at my age, and I pray the Lord will soon raise up a worldwide army of those whom the hymn describes: "Soldiers of Christ arise and put your armour on, strong in the strength which God supplies, through His eternal Son."[138]

I want to add, that although I have stated Satan can use unwary Christians in his service; even Peter was addressed by the Lord Jesus at one time saying to him "Get thee behind me Satan,"[139] and later Jesus told Peter when nearing His crucifixion that Satan had desired to sift him, Peter, as wheat but Jesus had prayed for him to eventually be restored and be able to strengthen his brethren,[140] faithful Christians, full of the Holy Spirit will be the last people on earth to become what in the Greek is called 'demonised'. But even these people of God can be overwhelmed in this way if, for instance, they persist in wilful deliberate sin or occult practices. Engaging in deliberate wilful sin, like pornography, can in fact lead to anyone becoming demonised. Thankfully, through repentance and faith and deliverance ministry these people can be restored to their full Christian heritage. Pornography in fact, can, like many other problems become addictive. I have found that addictions for e.g., alcohol or drugs can be caused by Satan, and deliverance ministry can set these people, and anyone else with addictions, completely free.

In closing what for me has been a difficult chapter to write, I would like to point out that anyone unwittingly engaging in an occult activity, like watching such on film, will not necessarily become demonised unless they persist in occult practices. I would add also that in the law given by God to Moses in the Old Testament, anyone being a medium, including one calling up the dead, had to be stoned to death as this is such a seriously evil practice in the eyes of God. I would urge all Christians to avoid séances or contact with clairvoyants and such people unless it is to minister deliverance to them, so that like the slave girl I have described in the Acts of the Apostles, they will lose all their supernatural abilities. I urge all Spirit endowed Christians always in their private devotions, and in church prayer meetings, to not only to pray powerfully, but to engage in spiritual warfare by authoritatively breaking the power of Satan over their nation and any of the parts of the world to which God may direct their prayers. It is to be remembered that when Jesus was tempted by the devil before he began His ministry, Satan offered to Him "all the Kingdoms of the World."[141] This indicates that the world at the present time is in the hands of Satan, hence all the evils that occur to mankind. But thankfully, the Bible states emphatically that when Jesus returns in glory "The kingdoms of this world shall become the kingdoms of God and of His Christ and He shall reign forever."[142] Maranatha Amen.

Chapter 19

Serving God in witnessing

What I have written could be criticised to some degree as too pietistic, involving solely an individual and their relationship with God. I make no apology for this however, as the very title of the book 'Walking with God' denotes clearly that this relationship, in all its aspects and in most of the experiences of life, is my task.

This relationship is of paramount importance according to the teaching of the Bible, including the Lord Jesus Christ Himself who said in a very important statement recorded in John's Gospel "And this is eternal life, that they may know You, the only true God, and Jesus Christ who You have sent."[143] So this relationship is seen to be of paramount importance for every living individual, and it encompasses the conditions to gain eternal life, not only in this world, but forevermore in glory. The words 'eternal life' used here in John's Gospel, in the Greek 'aiōnios zōē', has a present tense meaning: that this new quality of life in relationship with God is to be entered into at this present moment, not just to be experienced hereafter. Perhaps the old hymn gets it right when it says "Blessed assurance Jesus is mine, O what a foretaste of glory divine."[144]

137

So once again we see that this so-called pietistic relationship matters more than anything else in this world and the next. I must also explain that the word to 'know' used in this passage indicates not just a casual experience on the surface, it indicates the deepest possible relationship anyone can ever have with another. However, it is also true that Biblically this relationship is meant to spill over into contact and service with other people, even in what might be called 'secular society'.

Jesus teaches in the Sermon on the Mount, that the relationship of His followers with Him should mean, when it is as perfect as can be; that they are "the salt of the earth"[145], seasoning, as it were, the otherwise drastically incomplete life of humanity. Jesus also says that His people should be as lights in a dark place. He even says "You are the light of the world. A city set on a hill cannot be hid"[146] So Jesus teaches that without a relationship with Him, humanity and all its individuals are in darkness; they need the presence of Jesus' followers, who are keeping - as far as they perfectly can - Jesus' moral teachings from the Sermon on the Mount.

So we see that the so-called pietistic relationship with God was, however important, never meant to be an end in itself, but to spill out into the whole world. This teaching is further taken up by Jesus in the record of His last great prayer for His disciples on the night on which He was to be betrayed, as recorded by the Holy Spirit in what we know as John's Gospel. He prayed to the Father about His disciples, "I do not pray that they will be taken out of the world, but I pray that they will be kept from the evil one."[147]

In the Epistles, after describing how the death and resurrection of Jesus saved people from their sins, the Apostles do elaborate on the fact that Christians are still living in this world and that their life with God in Christ should make a very real difference to relationships, for example between man and wife, parents and children, and even slaves and their masters.[148] In the contemporary world therefore, Christians should have not only model homes and family life, not only fair and happy businesses in which they are engaging, but should also respect the rulers of their countries who are to be obeyed completely as they are appointed to their post by God Himself.

In my wide experience of Christianity and Christian believers, not only in my home country of the United Kingdom, but also in my world-wide travels, I have found sincere Christian people not only to be very fair to their employees when Christians are engaging in business and trade, but also I have found Christians to be engaged actively in the politics of their nation both nationally and on the local level and also to be very good headmasters and teachers in schools, and in fact, to engage with, as well-known Christians, the whole society in which they live. I have found such activities very much encouraged by all church leaders. Thus Christians are indeed following Jesus' command to be salt, seasoning the whole of human life; 'leaven' as Jesus said, to be leavening the whole loaf of human activity and indeed to be "light of the world."

It is very important to note that when the Risen Christ promised His disciples that they would receive power (Greek 'dunamis' - supernatural energy power) when they were to be baptised in the Holy Spirit, He said that the purpose of the receipt of this supernatural power by His people, for then and for all time, was to be "witnesses" to the reality of His Risen life.[149] We must say that a witness, even in a secular world, say a witness of a motor car accident, is a person who can describe events and happenings from his or her own experience. So, for instance, in modern society, when, for example the police appeal for witnesses, they do not want people who can only say "I heard about what happened from another person, who then told another person what happened, who told me." Such a person could not be a valid witness in any meaning of the word. So when Jesus said His disciples would receive the Holy Spirit of power to be "witnesses", He was saying that they should be able to speak from their own personal experience to describe, for instance, what God Himself, Father, Son or Holy Spirit had effectively done in their lives. A Christian witness therefore, is someone who does not merely go to church to share their experience with other Christians, but one who can boldly, yet humbly, say "I know from my own experience that God has completely changed my whole aspect on life." It is sad that many Christians, often when given the opportunity to say these words and explain the reality of God in their lives, may feel embarrassed, and just keep their lips sealed from any kind of witness. It is important to remember in this aspect of the Christians' service that Jesus said "Whoever confesses Me before men, him will I also confess before my Heavenly Father, but who is ashamed of Me before men, of him will I also be ashamed before My Heavenly Father."[150] So I pray for myself in in the words of this wonderful hymn: "Jesus, and shall it ever be, a mortal man ashamed of Thee? Ashamed of Thee, whom angles praise, whose glories shine through endless days? Ashamed of Jesus! Yes, I may when I've no guilt to wash away; no tear to wipe, no good to crave, no fears to quell, no soul to save. Till then nor is my boasting vain, till then I boast a Saviour slain; And O may this my glory be, that Christ is not ashamed of me!"[151]

In all this we see that a believers' deep relationship with God, which I have termed 'Walking with God', should not indeed be a solitary journey but one taken alongside other believers, and one which they as individuals or as a community spill out in action and service to the whole world. We as Christian believers must pray for every kind of work in society, that we feel God can bless, for instance

Christian Aid or Tear Fund which seek to alleviate hunger in the world, and such works as the Leprosy Mission which seek to provide medical assistance and indeed a cure for those not only suffering from this disease but other diseases also. I have named just two or three of the wonderful works being done by Christians throughout the world and in secular society. We could also include many others for example the Christian Monasteries who were the first Christian Hospitals caring for the sick and also sought to help the poor. People like Robert Raikes who started the first Sunday Schools for children who worked down the mines and thus began what was eventually to become free universal education for children in England. The Tolpuddle Martyrs established the first Christian Trade Unions in England and William Wilberforce was the first great activist as a member of the British Parliament to abolish the slave trade and of course Dr Barnardo who founded orphanages, and Lord Shaftesbury who championed social reform for the poor.

So again, if we ourselves are walking close with God we must, as overt Christians, undertake to pray for all humanity so that we fulfil Jesus' commission to be "light to the whole world", not in any way hiding our faith and light from men, but as it were in Jesus' words, setting a candlestick on a table to throw out its light to the whole of humanity. In essence, all this is about sheer unmerited love for our neighbours, loving them as God has loved us. Again Jesus commanded His disciples "Love one another as I have loved you and so shall you be my disciples,"[152] and His words "No man has greater love than this than that a man should lay down his life for a friend."[153] So the Christian church (Greek - called-out-ones) should live not for their own ends, or for their own gains, but to lay down their lives as Jesus did for the rest of humanity.

CONCLUSION

In the foregoing pages I have not in any way tried to set out dubious religious ideas or, any spiritual theories, and indeed in no way want to describe any future hopes for believers that cannot and will not be fulfilled. What I have tried to do in fact, is to set out solid uncontradictable Christian teaching covering the whole of a person's experience of life from teenager to being a senior citizen, and the relevance of scriptural teaching to each part. I have also tried to apply Christian teaching to several common experiences that people can encounter, usually causing hardship in their lives or minds, and I have sought to do this from my own experience of each one I describe, with the help I have received from God in these experiences, and all the time I have backed this up from experience and Christian teaching; I set out from what I regard as the infallible teachings from Holy Scripture.

In all, this is the fifteenth book I have had published and I want to state that I have in no way sought any financial gain from these often best-selling publications, as from the outset of my writings I have declared that all proceeds from the sale of my books will go into Christian work, especially now Crossbridge Books who has in fact published the very latest of my books that are available from them as indicated inside. My earnest prayer is that through my often inadequate writing, people may indeed find God in reality, as I described I found it after being an atheist, during a very traumatic mental illness. I also describe how persons who are genuinely seeking can find the reality of God in the Bible and in sharing life with God's people. I have also indicated how this experience of God can be deepened in communion with Him which I term 'Walking with God'.

I have also sought to explain how this communion with God can help all, through and beyond this life, through to our final destiny. It was my wife Anne's catechism to describe this as "enjoying God forever in Heaven." I hope people will be helped in some way from my writing into a deep relationship with God, and service for Him in the church, and in society. I write only in an inadequate way for the glory of God.

[1] Divine Healing, Deliverance, and the Kingdom of God
[2] 2 Corinthians 5:17
[3] Matthew 11:28
[4] Isaiah 40:31
[5] Jeremiah 29:11
[6] Isaiah 1:18-20
[7] Isaiah 26:3
[8] Genesis 1:1
[9] Genesis 1:26
[10] Psalm 56:11
[11] Psalm 103:2
[12] John 7:37
[13] John 4:14
[14] Matthew 11:28-30
[15] John 14:3
[16] 1 Peter 5:7
[17] Philippians 4:6-7
[18] Revelation 21:1-2
[19] Revelation 21:4
[20] Micah 4:3
[21] Jonah 1:17
[22] Daniel 5:5
[23] Numbers 22:28
[24] Ephesians 1:4
[25] 2 Timothy 3:16
[26] John 3:16
[27] Psalm 32:1-2
[28] Anonymous, 1837
[29] Luke 17:1-1
[30] Philippians 2:6
[31] John 13:5
[32] John 13:14
[33] John 15:12
[34] All praise to our redeeming Lord, Charles Wesley 1747
[35] Romans 3:23
[36] Romans 5:12; 1 Corinthians 15:21-22
[37] John 19:30
[38] 1 Peter 1:9
[39] 1 Peter 2:24

[40] Romans 8:2-4
[41] Ephesians 1:4
[42] John 3:1-3
[43] Luke 18:10-14
[44] John 3:16
[45] James 4:8
[46] Matthew 28:20
[47] Genesis 1:1
[48] 1Samuel 3:10
[49] John 10:4-5
[50] Hebrews 3:8
[51] Psalm 1:2
[52] Hebrews 4:12
[53] Ephesians 6:17
[54] Isaiah 26:3
[55] 1 Corinthians 9:27
[56] Acts 17:22-28
[57] Matthew 1:23
[58] Matthew 9:9
[59] John 4:20
[60] John 4:24
[61] Revelation 3:20
[62] Isaiah 57:15
[63] James 4:8
[64] Matthew 10:30
[65] Deuteronomy 33:27
[66] John 14:3-16; 16:4-11
[67] Romans 8:26
[68] John 3:1-21
[69] Galatians 5:22-23
[70] 1 Corinthians 6:19-20
[71] Acts of the Apostles 1:8
[72] Albert Orsborn 1886-1967
[73] 1 Corinthians 7:14
[74] Matthew 18:3
[75] 1 Peter 2:9
[76] 1 Corinthians 3:6
[77] 1 Corinthians 7:32-34
[78] Matthew 5:48; Leviticus 19:2

[79] Matthew 5:14-16
[80] Matthew 27:46
[81] Genesis 1:31
[82] 2 Corinthians 1:4
[83] Revelation 21:4
[84] Matthew 6:28
[85] Matthew 6:33
[86] Matthew 6:25-27
[87] Isaiah 25:3
[88] John 14:27
[89] Philippians 4:7
[90] 1 Peter 5:7
[91] Psalm 1:1-2
[92] Hebrews 4:12
[93] John 5:6
[94] Romans 7:19-20
[95] Romans 3:23
[96] Matthew 25:14-21
[97] Ephesians 2:8
[98] Isaiah 52:12
[99] Romans 8:37
[100] Mark 4:38-41
[101] John Flavel (1627-1691) born Bromsgrove; 1 Corinthians 1:8-11
[102] William Whiting (1860)
[103] Philippians 3:13-14
[104] Charles Wesley (1738)
[105] 1 Corinthians 15:53-55
[106] 2 Corinthians 5:1
[107] Acts 26:13
[108] Matthew 10:8
[109] Titus 1:1
[110] Luke 4:8; Deuteronomy 6:13
[111] Robert Grant (1833)
[112] Ephesians 5:18-19
[113] Laurie Klein (1978)
[114] 1 Corinthians 23-26
[115] Walter Chalmers Smith (1824-1908)
[116] Cleland Boyd McAfee (1903)
[117] John 4:24

[118] 1 Corinthians 12:27
[119] Ephesians 4:11
[120] 1 Corinthians 12:7-11
[121] John 4:17-18
[122] John 4:29
[123] Luke 20:25
[124] 1 Kings 4:29-34
[125] 1 Corinthians 12:1-6
[126] 1 Corinthians 12:30-31
[127] 1 Peter 5:8
[128] Ephesians 6:12
[129] Ephesians 6:11
[130] Acts of the Apostles 13:8
[131] Acts of the Apostles 13:12
[132] Acts of the Apostles 16:16
[133] Acts of the Apostles 16:19-24
[134] Romans 1:26-27
[135] Ephesians 1:21
[136] 1 Samuel 28:7
[137] 1 Samuel 28:19
[138] Charles Wesley (1749)
[139] Mark 8:33
[140] Luke 22:31-32
[141] Matthew 4:8
[142] Revelation 11:15
[143] John 17:3
[144] Fanny Crosby (1820-1915)
[145] Matthew 5:13
[146] Matthew 5:14
[147] John 17:15
[148] 1 Peter 2:11-25; 3:1-7
[149] Acts of the Apostles 1:8
[150] Luke 9:26
[151] Joseph Grigg (1765)
[152] John 15:12
[153] John 15:13